Working Abroad in Higher Education

If Only I Knew?

Working Abroad in Higher Education

If Only I Knew?

Dr. Michael Clarke

PARTRIDGE

A Penguin Random House Company

To order additional copies of this book, contact
Toll Free 800 101 2657 (Singapore)
Toll Free 1 800 81 7340 (Malaysia)
orders.singapore@partridgepublishing.com

www.partridgepublishing.com/singapore

Contents

Acknowledgements

I am greatly indebted to all those expatriate academics that participated in this research study. Dr. Robin Shields, Dr. Helen Verhoeven and Dr. Esinath Ndiweni provided valuable insights and contributions throughout this research study. I wish to thank you all for your time and support. Sharon Ang greatly assisted me in putting this book together – thank you for your persistence and eye for detail.

This book is dedicated to the Clarke family – my mum and dad, brothers and sister, sisters-in-law, cousins and my son.

Glossary

AUQA	Australian Universities Quality Agency
CAA	Commission for Academic Accreditation
EPSRC	Engineering and Physical Sciences Research Council
FE/HE	Further Education/Higher Education
HE	Higher Education
HEFCE	Higher Education Funding Council for England
HEM	Higher Education Management
HERA	Higher Education Role Analysis
HRM	Human Resource Management
IBC	International Branch Campus
IT	Information Technology
ICT	Information and Communications Technology
KHDA	Knowledge and Human Development Authority
KTP	Knowledge Transfer Partnerships
OBHE	The Observatory on Borderless Higher Education
OECD	The Organisation for Economic Co-operation and Development
QAA	Quality Assurance Agency
RAE	Research Assessment Exercise
REF	Research Excellence Framework
UAE	United Arab Emirates
UNESCO	The United Nations Educational, Scientific and Cultural Organization
UQAIB	University Quality Assurance International Board
VLE	Virtual Learning Environment

Abstract

Rapid expansion of the transnational higher education market has occurred over the past two decades (Altbach and Knight, 2007). Consequently, this expansion has led to an increased mobility of academics, but few research studies have investigated their experiences (Knight, 2011, 2013). Knight (2013) argued that more research is required in order to understand the challenges, complexities and environment which are faced by overseas academics. This research study investigated the professional role of fourteen British expatriate academics who are currently working at three British branch campuses operating in the United Arab Emirates (UAE). Currently, the UAE hosts the largest percentage of the world's International Branch Campuses.

The key findings of this study highlight that there are significant challenges in the nature of the academic role in the core areas of teaching, research and administration. The findings of this research also suggest that the academic role in a transnational higher education environment is more challenging than their previous UK experiences given the type of students that they teach and the University environmental setting.

This study has gone one step further based on the current literature in prioritising challenges that have the greatest impact on academics working overseas. It was found that expatriate academics are faced with considerable challenges in settling into their overseas position, as there is often little or no support, provided for induction or mentoring systems in place. Another key finding of this research is that overseas academics perceive that it would be very difficult to return to the UK Higher Education sector. Several recommendations have been put forward to address the aforementioned challenges.

Chapter 1

INTRODUCTION

1.1 The Context of this Study

Over the past two decades, educational researchers have observed the rapid expansion of transnational higher education activity (Altbach 2002; Chapman and Pyvis 2006; Altbach and Knight 2007; Naidoo 2009). The increase and growth of transnational higher education has led to an increased international mobility of academics (Altbach 2002). Robson (2001) and Knight (2011) have observed that there have been few research studies undertaken on the experiences of academics that work and live abroad. They suggest that extensive research work is required in order to understand these challenges and the overseas environment which are faced by academics. Richardson and McKenna (2002) provide some useful evidence indicating that there were difficulties experienced in their study of thirty British expatriate academics that were working in Turkey, Singapore, New Zealand and the United Arab Emirates. The authors cite, "the expatriate can be seen as an explorer in that taking an overseas position presented an opportunity both to explore another culture and to undertake this exploration in an independent way through living and learning a new culture." (p.7). Although this may not be the major focus of Richardson and McKenna (2002) study, but they stated challenges of settling-in, difficulties faced in applying teaching pedagogy and cultural adjustment in moving to a new country. Chapman and Austin (2002) have argued for greater attention and resource to be provided for expatriate academics working overseas on their recruitment, training and support.

For many overseas academics, teaching multi-cultural students, dealing with poor English language skills and working with a

1

standardised curriculum (i.e. same materials and assessments) appear to be stumbling blocks and present challenges in the classroom setting (Bodycott and Walker, 2000). Bodycott and Walker (2000) conducted their study in Hong Kong based on their own teaching observations. They argue that expatriate academics are ill-prepared to teach in overseas branch campuses as so often academics are unaware of pedagogical strategies to cope with students who have never learnt critical thinking in their previous schooling system. Very limited research is conducted in overseas branch campuses. Richardson and Zikic (2007) suggest that the main reason for this is that academics have been encumbered with high teaching loads, which prevents them from pursuing research. Fielden and Gillard (2011) conducted research at nine overseas branch campuses on staffing strategies and suggested that the main purpose of the private sector university was mainly focused on teaching. Research was very limited throughout the overseas campuses visited.

The next section will discuss the aims and expected contributions that this study aims to make in the area of the academic role in an overseas setting.

1.2 The Aims and Expected Contribution of this Study

Several researchers identified that there were limited studies on the premise of 'players' involved working at overseas branch campuses (Robson 2001; Knight 2011). The aim of this study is to examine the professional role of British expatriate academics working at UAE branch campuses. Therefore, the primary research question for this study is:

How do the overseas conditions and environment affect the professional role of the British expatriate academic?

The contribution of this study deems significance to several stakeholders. Firstly, it will be of interest for those British academics that are exploring the opportunity to work overseas in transnational higher education. Is it attractive to British academics to work abroad? British expatriate academics are investigated in terms of their decision on moving to work overseas, about their experiences in their role and how it compares to working previously in the UK Higher Education (HE, hereafter) sector. Other questions addressed in this study concerns how their role overseas affects their career aspirations and insights into how the overseas branches operate can be useful to access the working conditions that expatriate academics work in. Secondly, such research is useful for senior managers of overseas branch campuses to assess the implications and recommendations that are gathered from research outcomes of the study. Thirdly, senior managers based at home campuses can understand and appreciate the conditions that academics operate in and can influence necessary decisions to ensure that the British branch campuses are improved to enhance the overall student learning experience. The next section outlines the structure of the study.

1.3 Structure of the Research Study

Chapter Two constitutes the literature review, which is split into three major parts. Firstly, Part One of the Chapter begins with a discussion on the changing UK academic landscape and how neoliberal forces have shaped the nature of the UK HE sector and have impacted on the professional role of the academic. It is important to discuss the UK HE sector as several themes in this fieldwork asked respondents on how their experiences of working overseas compare to their experiences of working previously in the UK HE sector. Several areas within Part One are relevant to transnational higher education particularly the sections on ICT, internationalisation, graduate employability, marketisation and regulation as they negatively affect the curriculum.

The second part of Chapter Two explains the growth of transnational higher education due to factors such as globalisation, IT infrastructure and the need for Western universities to seek out new income streams due to government funding cuts. I further delve deeper into identifying challenges faced by overseas academics based on the research studies and literature available on International Higher Education. These are categorised into four broad areas: (a) country, institutional, cultural and market challenges (b) Higher Education as a global commodity (c) quality and perceptual issues and (d) challenges in teaching, research and administration.

3

In Part Three of Chapter Two, I present a useful framework (Framework of Five Essential Elements, Gappa et al 2007) alongside a study by Chapman et al (2014), which was recently conducted in UAE public and semi-public universities. The study by Chapman et al (2014) applied the same Framework of Five Essential Elements (Gappa et al. 2007) as in my study. The recent QAA UAE Overseas Transnational Review of Higher Education (2014) is examined alongside country specific discussion of the UAE Higher Education system. A summary is provided, of literature comparison of the UK and overseas academic roles in terms of teaching, research and administrative as it is particularly relevant to this research study. The final section in this Chapter identifies the research gap.

Chapter Three discusses the research design for this study that was undertaken in the UAE and how it was chosen and conducted. The researcher provides justification of employed methods and the interpretative stance taken using qualitative data. The researcher has conducted fourteen in-depth semi-structured interviews at three British Universities which have overseas campuses based in the UAE. The criterion for selection was that the expatriate academics must have held previous teaching experience in UK higher education. The three British Universities have been unidentified and given a pseudonym. This was also applied to the fourteen respondents who were interviewed in this study. Interview transcripts were transcribed totalling 77,000 words based upon 632 minutes of recorded interview time and imported into NVivo for coding and analysis.

In Chapter Four, the study presents findings and results of the fieldwork data alongside the themes set out in Chapter Three. The study provides discussion and several recommendations based on the result findings produced in Chapter Five.

In the Conclusion (Chapter Six), the research draws together the outcomes in the context of the original research questions. This study provides knowledge contribution that has been made to the literature and new insights into this field of work in transnational higher education. Finally, the research presents possible further studies that will contribute to advance the understanding and knowledge of working in transnational higher education.

Chapter 2

LITERATURE REVIEW

2.1 Introduction

In the first part of this Chapter, the literature explores the changes that have occurred in the UK higher education sector over the past several decades and examines how they have affected the academic profession. The literature highlights how this relates to the context of transnational higher education particularly in relation to the delivery of a standardised curriculum. I begin section 2.2 by explaining the changing UK academic landscape, which has become heavily influenced by the UK government. Section 2.2 examines the massification of the UK higher education sector, which has significantly increased the participation rates of young people securing their first degree. One of the major impacts on the academic professional role is teaching larger class sizes and their subsequent effects on teaching pedagogy, teaching to a greater diversity of students and pressures of increased workload.

Increased government accountability and scrutiny is discussed in section 2.3. Two government bodies have particularly impacted the academic community. The Quality Assurance Agency was set up to improve academic standards. This section discusses how this Agency has increased administration duties undertaken by academics and subsequently has led to reducing the autonomy once held by the academic community. The Research Assessment Exercise has also had a major impact on controlling the type of research expected of the academe. Research output has now become the normal route in the UK for academic promotion. Section 2.4 explores how power has shifted from the academe to senior administrators. It will also examine the impact of new human resource practices, which has led to individual scrutiny of the academic profession. Section 2.5 reflects upon the growing importance of the student as a consumer and how it affects academics under a new complaint system and increased external monitoring. The growth of international students taking up admissions in the UK is examined in section 2.6. It discusses new challenges that academics face in their teaching pedagogy due to language and learning style differences. Section 2.7 explores the UK government's agenda to produce a curriculum geared towards graduate employability and how this further reduces academic autonomy. Section 2.8 examines how there has been an increase in part-time academic staff in the HE sector in order to meet fluctuations in student demand and help towards balancing reduced University budgets. The impact of new technology and entrepreneurialism are examined in sections 2.9 and 2.10 respectively.

The second part of this Chapter explores the growth of transnational higher education and its impact on the professional role of the expatriate academic working in this field. Part Two begins firstly by explaining the reasons why this provision has grown rapidly over the past two decades exploring a number of contributory factors that have shaped and fuelled its growth. Concurrently, increased academic mobility has occurred as a result of this growth (Knight, 2013). Section 2.13 examines the key challenges and issues facing transnational higher education. According to Knight (2013), these present different challenges compared to those academics working at Western Universities. Section 2.14 examines country, institutional, cultural and market challenges. This section is important, as it highlights a number of challenges that expatriate academics are facing such as lack of pre-departure or cultural training that often causes stress and anxiety both inside and outside the classroom. Section 2.15 suggests that there are often perceptual issues that affect the quality of transnational higher education. Part of these issues is caused by distance and relationships between the host and home campuses; part of it is caused by limited resourcing, cultural misunderstandings etc. Issues are also caused by the academic perception of international students who perform worse than home-based students. All these conditions affect the academic working in the overseas environment. Section 2.16 examines the literature that has been written to-date on overseas teaching, research and administration. It reveals that there is limited research being undertaken by expatriate academics, they have increased teaching loads and are challenged in their administrative duties. In addition, expatriate academics are also faced with great difficulty in teaching overseas students. Hofstede's (1986) contribution on learning and teaching has proven to be very informative on this issue and a number of academic views have been presented in this section.

The final part of this Chapter begins with an important framework in section 2.17. The researcher has used Gappa et al (2007) Framework of Essential Elements to form part of his interview questions given that it relates to the professional role of the academic. I provide reasons for its selection and usefulness to this research. Recent research has been applied using this framework to explain its application within the UAE. This has been applied to both federal and semi-public Universities in the UAE but has not yet been conducted in private sector Universities. Part Three discusses the growth and nature of the UAE Higher Education sector in section 2.18 and captures the more recent findings of the QAA UAE Transnational Review in section 2.19. This report was recently conducted in 2014 and is important to explain the quality of British University provision in the UAE as there are currently over 15,000 students taking a British degree programme.

The final section of Part Three examines some of the key differences and similarities between the professional roles of the British academic in comparison to those academics working in a transnational higher education institution. This is derived from critically reviewing the literature discussed in Parts One and Two of this Chapter. Section 2.20 identifies that expatriate academics focus largely on teaching and administration in comparison to British academics. In addition, recent literature suggests that whilst teaching has become more challenging in the UK as a result of the changes in the UK HE sector, teaching in an overseas environment can also be challenging given cultural misunderstandings and adjustment in teaching pedagogy. The researcher summarises these differences and similarities in table 2.1. A summary of the literature on issues and challenges facing expatriate academics is presented in Appendix Six. Section 2.21 discusses the research gap from the literature, which is important in developing the research aim and design in Chapter Three.

PART ONE

2.2 The Changing UK Academic Landscape

Most of the changes that have impacted the global HE sector over the past five decades have been influenced to a large extent by national governments (Waring, 2010). Waring, (2010) cites, "the response of national governments has been largely informed and driven by the ideology of neoliberalism, leading to a process of change characterised by modernisation" (p. 59). In the UK, the HE sector has been transformed into becoming a more "business focused" entity resulting from the trends in the massification of HE, tighter government regulation, reducing resources and the opening up of the sector to marketisation and competition (Locke and Bennion 2007; Doring, 2002; Dearlove 2002; Anderson 1998; Huisman et al 2002; Becher and Trowler 2011; Callender and Scott 2013; Waring 2010; Gappa et al 2007; Mayhew et al 2004; Wilmott 1995; Scott 2000; Welch 1998). This section discusses the changes that have occurred, their implications for the sector and how they have affected the nature of the UK academic profession.

2.3 Massification of the UK Higher Education Sector

There has been a significant increase in the number of students entering Higher Education. This has been driven by the UK's goal of achieving 50% of young people obtaining a degree (Dearlove, 2002). The government's agenda has been focused in improving the UK's economy and performance by developing a knowledge-based economy and raising higher skills levels. For the University, they have had to move away from teaching students in smaller to larger class sizes. Academics have had to adjust their teaching pedagogy in terms of their teaching practice (e.g. use of video clips or additional student readings), adapting new assessment strategy and learning methods. According to Dearlove (2002), "mass higher education has reduced control over student entry. A rising tide of vocationalism has pushed new skills into the curriculum against the wishes of many academics", (p. 262). Locke and Bennion (2007) were involved in producing a large-scale survey of academics that compared and contrasted findings between the 1992 and the 2007 academic surveys and found that teaching hours per week fell between the two periods. However, class sizes were considerably higher which has implications for providing additional student support and increased assessment marking. Some of the research, which studied the change factors (larger class sizes), in both the UK and Australia suggested that academics are disengaging from their previous change agent roles that was once dominated by "interaction and dialogue" by teaching in smaller class sizes (p. 139). Doring (2002), Waring (2010) and Mayhew et al (2004) are very critical of teaching increased class sizes. Waring (2010) suggests from his research findings that staff workload has increased due to the effects of massification. Coupled with the reduction per unit cost allocated by the government for student teaching, this has had the effect of commodifying academic work. In addition, Waring argues that greater diversity of students creates added pressures and complexities to academic teaching. Waring posits, "academics may be seen to be losing ideological control of their work under the pressure of marketisation and massification in HE", (p. 51).

2.4 Tighter Government Legislation

Prior to the 1960s, collegiality was the norm and academics monitored their own teaching and research. Nowadays, the government is interventionist. Two quasi-government bodies, the Quality Assurance Agency (QAA) and the Research Councils were initiated to increase government accountability to improve academic standards and research output in the sector. There has been greater scrutiny of activities and in meeting standards placed upon the Higher Education sector at both home and abroad (Shore and Wright, 2000). As a result, Universities have become more bureaucratic and more accountable to bodies such as the QAA and the Research Assessment Exercise (RAE). "A study of the implications of quality assessment and quality assurance policies finds that higher education institutions are responding to current pressures with policies and structures that draw substantially on post-bureaucratic or "new public management" thinking. In contrast with the course of study there are many academics who are struggling with values and concepts of professional practice that are traditionally dependent on pre-modern form of governance and organisation" (Henkel, 1997, p.134). Henkel (1997) studied the policy reforms in the UK, Sweden and Norway and how it had affected academics. He found that academics were increasing their administration duties. In addition, the University administration function became much more structured developing more rules, regulations and procedures. Henkel posits, "many academics expressed bitter resentment at the weight and type of administration in this complex of activities: the documentation required to conform to the new quality assurance systems, triggered by external audit and assessment was a prime target" (p. 141). Altbach (2009) reinforces Henkel's view that academics have lost a lot of their autonomy and control over their teaching and research. He argues that assessment exercises take time for academics to complete and that academics must also become much more productive in producing research.

According to Waring (2010), the UK HE sector has transformed itself towards an audit culture where regulatory bodies have impacted the role of academic work that is levered by accountability. New layers of management have been introduced in controlling processes and procedures that are similar to the transition that occurred in the National Health sector. Academics have had to submit themselves to audit scrutiny and a reduction in their academic autonomy. He posits, "academics and other knowledge workers require the freedom, autonomy and high levels of discretion to operate effectively. Continual attempts to erode such conditions not only lead to confusion and uncertainty for academics but ultimately risks damaging the core of the academy itself", (p.279). The research by Waring also confirms that academics are consuming more of their time in their preparation for inspections and audits. Academics also had increased workload as a result of teaching larger class sizes linked to more assessment marking. His research confirmed that academics were focusing their research on safe research projects rather than pursuing original research (similar to the Dearlove 2002 finding). The key criterion nowadays for academic promotion is via quality research output in the UK. This confirms

Locke and Bennion (2007) finding indicating that the level of research interest grew by 9% over the 15-year period (1992 to 2007). Academics have re-prioritised their focus of work onto research that is practical (Doring, 2002).

2.5 Managerialism and Individualism

Managerialism has become incorporated into the UK Higher Education sector. New academic posts have been created to implement business and human resource practices to bring about changes in driving economy and efficiency into the sector. According to Becher and Trowler (2011), this has affected greater scrutiny of the academic role and in meeting standards. What is noticeable is that the power has shifted away from the academe to senior administrators (Becher and Trowler, 2011). Many academics have been critical of these changes in their research. They state, "To generalise, de-professionalization of academic life is occurring, while traditional ideas about the special status and knowledge claims of academics have rapidly become outdated" (p. 13). Altbach (2009) posits, "if professors cannot devote their full attention not only to teaching and research but also to maintaining an academic culture, working with students outside the classroom and participating in the governance of their universities, academic quality will decline. As the British say, "penny wise and pound foolish" (p. 16). To Altbach, these practices are counter-productive as academics are the core people who contribute to the success of Higher Education. Callender and Scott (2013) argue that managerialism has embedded key performance indicators into HE institutions and has eroded collegiality and trust. According to Henkel (1997), these initiatives have led to "open the black box" of academic decision-making and shifted power away to the central administration unit. The UK survey findings (produced by Locke and Bennion, 2007) indicate that academics felt disengagement in the running of their universities and are "alienated from leadership" (p.36). They argue, "academic self-governance has been weakened, the influence of academic senate has declined and the academic community seemingly marginalised as a consequence" (p.36). Waring (2010) argues that managerialism has had the overall effect of eroding the collegial tradition and the very status and individualism of the academic profession. He argues that such a 'homogeneous strategy' cannot be applied to a sector that is highly complex in nature.

UK Universities have introduced human resource management (HRM) practices over the past ten years to enhance control over academics (Waring, 2010). The research by Waring investigated the extent of how HRM strategies have affected the role of the academic. His conclusions suggest that academic work cannot be reduced easily to specific performance criteria or become routine. "As a consequence, academics who used to enjoy high degrees of autonomy and the ability to effectively manage themselves, now find that freedom significantly curtailed by a process of individualisation" (p.89). Deem (2004) argues that managing academic work is not the same or comparable to managing retail businesses or industrial production and can be more challenging (p. 111). Dearlove (2002) on the other hand suggests that the changes made to the UK HE sector were necessary in serving the needs of society. Rather than looking at the past he argues that academics must adopt managerialism combining this with collegiality by working with the administrative function to develop a shared vision and implement University strategy together. He argues that academics are "as hard to herd as cats" which is the key reason why both academics and administrators have no other choice but to work together (Dearlove, 2002, p.268). He is supportive of the view that University departments can hold enormous power within an institution to block or implement strategy. By devolving control to Deans, they are in a better position to manage the divide that exists between the academic and administrative bodies.

2.6 Marketisation and the Student as a Customer

The introduction of student fees in 1998 meant that the UK Higher Education sector has had to change their culture and their approach to treating students as 'customers' (Becher and Trowler, 2011). The Browne reforms recently implemented in 2012/13 has had a major impact upon the restructuring and funding of the UK HE sector leading to full marketisation (Callender and Scott, 2013). Student fee levels for the home students rose to £9,000 per year for undergraduate programmes that opened up market competition in the UK HE sector. "For HE institutions this has meant high levels of competition, scarce resources and new associated costs, as well as unpredictable fluctuations in enrolments and revenues" (Becher and Trowler, 2011, p. 1). Complaints systems and student league tables have become a feature of the UK Higher Education sector and these have led to a shift towards the power of the student body (Becher and Trowler, 2011). Parker and Jary (1995) go as far as suggesting that Universities are creating the 'McUniversity' in an attempt to become more student-friendly. This has affected the academe in that there is greater scrutiny of their activities and in meeting standards. Naidoo (2003) argues that academics may refrain from innovation in teaching due to the culture of student litigation and complaints alongside external monitoring procedures. Locke and Bennion (2007) indicated that there was an overall 2% drop in job satisfaction in their study findings between 1992 and 2007.

If Universities in the UK are deferring their innovation in teaching (Naidoo, 2003), then this raises concerns also for overseas branch campuses in the case of applying similar teaching materials, assessments and learning outcomes. This will further be discussed in Part Two of this Chapter.

2.7 Internationalisation

According to Becher and Trowler (2011), the Higher Education sector has become much more globalised as a result of the fiscal constraints imposed by governments and this has led to a significant increase of international students entering the UK to pursue HE programmes and the growth of transnational higher education (both face-to-face and online). This has created the necessity for developing a more internationalised curriculum for both home and overseas providers and for academics to adapt their teaching pedagogy to varying student ability levels (Locke and Bennion, 2007, p.20). The study findings conducted by Locke and Bennion (2007) reveal that vast majority of British academics have never worked or studied abroad (p.20). They argue that the lack of international exposure has negative consequences for developing a truly internationalised curriculum and those academics will be challenged in teaching international students although it is interesting that 27% of full-time academic staff who work in the UK come from non-UK countries. According to Forest (2010), the key to improving an international curriculum is to convince the academe to adopt an international focus in their teaching and research. In his survey of 20,000 academics worldwide, the findings reflect that researchers are more interested in global connections than to academics that only teach. This has implications for producing global knowledge in the classroom, "... teaching professors hold relatively insular views regarding curriculum development" (p.448). Forest (2010) puts forward a recommendation to have home-based teachers go abroad to teach in transnational Colleges and Universities. There are very few studies that address academics that teach international students. Daniels (2012) survey of 140 academic staff found that academics lacked the support in teaching international students and were challenged. The study also revealed that English language followed by learning style differences of international students were the major issues affecting student learning. Trahar and Hyland (2011) applied a small-scale focus group across five English universities looking at the experiences of home-based staff and international students. Their findings revealed problems in the lack of intercultural interaction and difficulties with particular classroom pedagogy such as group work (p. 623).

The literature above is important as it raises questions on the relevancy of an internationalised curriculum if academics that produce these materials for overseas campuses do not have the experience of working abroad themselves. How would they know what is best practice? This will be explored in Part Two of this Chapter.

2.8 Graduate Employability

According to Locke and Bennion (2007), there has been an increasing pressure by the UK government to focus University efforts on producing a curriculum geared towards graduate employability by addressing skills outputs and forging closer links to industry. It has been the government's agenda to improve the UK economy by enhancing higher-order skills base levels. Whilst these are notable initiatives, it has not proved to be effective according to Storen and Aamodt (2010). Their research examined 36,000 graduates in thirteen European countries who had graduated at least five years previously. Their findings show that their degree undertaken did not help the graduates secure a job itself but it allowed them to perform better in the job role. The degrees that were vocationally based had the greatest impact on work performance. The implications of this research clearly indicate the need to modify the curriculum. Mason et al (2009) conducted research into students, academics and career staff and also found that prior work experience provided the highest factor in obtaining a job. Hinchliffe and Jolly (2011) conducted their research into examining what employees expected from graduates. Their findings are similar to Mason et al (2009) in that employees wanted graduates to have previous work experience or volunteering roles, which allowed students to step out of their 'comfort zones'. Hinchliffe and Jolly (2011) refer to this as the "graduate identity" (p. 581). There has been much criticism on how this government agenda has affected the academic profession. Boden and Epstein (2006) argue that Universities have been reduced to being "knowledge production factories" due to government policy (p.225). Waring (2010) has been very critical of government initiatives citing that "academics and other knowledge workers require the freedom, autonomy and high levels of discretion to operate effectively. Continued attempts to erode such conditions not only lead to confusion and uncertainty for academics" (p. 279).

This section highlights that introducing graduate employability into the national curriculum has clearly influenced the UK professional academic role. However, when it comes to implementing a standardised curriculum abroad, it raises fundamental questions if can fit in the context of the overseas graduate market as each country will vary in nature. This will be discussed further in Part Two of this Chapter.

2.9 Growth of part-time and fixed-term appointments

There has been substantial growth of part-time and fixed-term appointments in the UK that has been influenced by the need for flexibility to meet fluctuating student demand and reduced budgets (Gappa et al, 2007). According to Gappa et al (2007), part-timers do not feel part of the academic community and are often prevented from participating in their respective institutions or benefitting from professional growth in comparison to their full-time colleagues. These factors underlie the very nature of work satisfaction. Gappa et al (2007) suggest that by incorporating part-timers into the institution and by valuing and respecting them 'as assets' will immensely benefit and improve the institution and the overall student learning experience. "These elements are the glue that bonds the individual faculty member and the college or university together in a mutually rewarding reciprocal relationship" (p. 37).

The utilisation of part-time staff has also been used extensively in transnational higher education to drive down costs and improve flexibility (Gappa et al, 2007). This study will investigate how this affects the expatriate academic.

2.10 New Technology

ICT has changed teaching pedagogy and impacted on the role of the academe. (Locke and Bennion, 2007). Academics have faced difficulties in adapting to this new style of teaching. It also raises implications for academics where their contact with students may move outside the traditional working day. The up-take of technology has also jointly coincided alongside globalisation that has meant that larger Universities are now capable to offer their degree programmes worldwide via online learning platforms, which do not require attendance at local campuses (Becher and Trowler, 2011). The introduction of improved technology (VLE and on-line library databases) has helped support the growth of transnational higher education. This will further be discussed in Part Two of this Chapter.

2.11 Entrepreneurialism

There has been increased movement by UK Universities to enhance income via entrepreneurial activity as a result of reduced government budgets and fluctuating student enrolments e.g. training for industry, patents, consultancy, Knowledge Transfer Partnerships (KTPs), overseas markets and spin-out companies etc. (Dearlove 2002; Becher and Trowler 2011). According to Waring (2010), Universities have developed business units that stress upon the financial management and monitoring of individual academic performance via the performance appraisal system. Scott (2000) posits that Universities "have become big corporate bureaucracies. In almost every sense, the University has been transformed" (p. 8). For the academic, this has presented themselves with new opportunities for personal and professional development or challenges in coping with this new commercial activity.

It is also noted that increased reliance on UK University funding has helped fuel the growth of transnational higher education which will be discussed in Part Two of this Chapter.

2.12 Part One Summary

There is no doubt from the literature presented that the academic profession has changed over the past five decades due to the changing environmental landscape. According to Locke and Bennion (2007), "there is evidence of shifts in the balance between teaching and research and of the changing conceptions of scholarship and professional responsibilities" (p.45). The emergence of 'managerialism', 'marketisation' and 'massification' raise a number of key questions for those potential candidates seeking scholarly careers at a time when permanent academic careers are shrinking. Locke and Bennion (2007) conclude that, "broader challenges, to professional authority and academic autonomy, have also contributed to a reconfiguration of academic identities" (p.47). Critical voices reflect the increase of management practices that have the effect of limiting academic decision-making and lowering expectations of collegiality. Doring (2002) argues that the external changes discussed earlier 'devalue' teaching. This view is shared by Willmott (1995) who examined and applied Weber's theory to the academic profession and found that academic work had become commodified. The research by Waring (2010) clearly highlights that academics have lost much of their control over teaching and research. They have become scrutinised and monitored under formalised performance appraisal systems.

Schapper and Mayson (2004) argue that commoditisation of the curriculum (i.e. same curriculum, same materials and same learning outcomes) has the effect of deskilling academic staff who work overseas. There are similarities arising between the two sets of literature on how change affects the academic professional role. This will be discussed in Part Two.

PART TWO

2.13 The Growth of Transnational Higher Education

This next section discusses the growth of transnational higher education over the past two decades and will explain how the environmental factors have shaped and influenced this phenomenon. Naidoo (2007) defines transnational higher education to cover franchising, twinning degrees, branch campuses, distance learning, degree articulations and corporate degrees (e.g. IBM and Motorola). These are delivered outside the home country awarding body. Transnational higher education has grown rapidly over the past two decades (Naidoo 2009; Chapman and Pyvis 2006; Bennell and Pearce 2003). This growth has been concentrated in the Middle East, Asia and Eastern European regions. Concurrently, academic employment has also seen an expansion (Knight, 2013).

In 1997, there were approximately between 135,000 and 140,000 students taking UK degrees outside the UK. This figure has risen to over 500,000 students in 2012 and has now surpassed the number of international students entering the UK to pursue their degrees (Lawton et al, Observatory of Higher Education, 2013). The British Council predicts that this trend will continue to expand up until 2020 but at a much slower rate compared to the previous two decades. The UK is not the only country involved in transnational higher education. According to Naidoo (2009), transnational higher education represents 33% (Australia), 25% (New Zealand) and 20% (USA) of each country's service sector export respectively. Naidoo (2003) suggests that due to the overall government funding cuts placed on these Western Universities as discussed in Part One, this has resulted in the need to seek out alternative sources of income elsewhere. This has been one of the key contributory factors which has influenced the growth of transnational higher education. At the same time, governments in developing countries are facing difficulties in financing higher education themselves. "The inability of governments to mobilise resources for higher education and the rebranding of higher education as an exportable commodity has led to a stampede by private for-profit providers" (Naidoo, 2003, p.252). Developing country governments recognise the need and importance to invest in higher education and if properly regulated can serve as a creative, efficient and cost effective means to meet student demand (Bennell and Pearce 2003; Chapman and Austin 2002).

Globalisation is the process of integrated internationalisation that derives from the emergence of ideas, products and the influences of culture (Salmi, 2002). He argues that the enabling factors which advance globalisation, include the development of transportation, communication (internet and telecommunications) and economic trade. According to Salmi (2002), globalisation has affected everyone in the world and in every country. He cites, "economic development is increasingly linked to a nation's ability to acquire and apply technical socioeconomic knowledge, and the process of globalisation is accelerating this trend" (p.25). Salmi (2002) posits that barriers have been lifted to access information and communication between "people, institutions and countries" (p.26). Globalisation has fuelled the growth of transnational higher education. For Western Universities involved in transnational higher education; they are also able to achieve global presence and branding. There is also significant growth in distance learning programmes as a result of much improved technology and on-line library database infrastructure (Salmi, 2002) as discussed in Part One. Universities, according to Scott (2000), "have essentially been tied to national cultures. E-learning standardises teaching and opens up new fronts for modern Universities called corporate universities" (p.8). Institutions such as Laureate, Kaplan, University of Phoenix have taken advantage of on-line technologies to deliver their teaching pedagogy. Multimedia technology has changed pedagogical approaches to student learning. "Combining online and regular classroom courses gives students more opportunity for human interaction and development of the social aspects of learning through direct communication, argumentation, discussion, and consensus building" (Salmi, 2002, p.35).

2.14 Transnational Higher Education – Challenges and Issues

There are several studies that have discussed the key challenges and issues facing transnational higher education. In investigating these, this will help to understand and explain the environmental factors and conditions in which academics are currently working in overseas higher education. According to Knight (2013), "the complexities and challenges related to academic and profession mobility should not be underestimated" (p.87).

The following areas have been categorised into the key influential concerns impacting the transnational higher education landscape:

(a) Country, Institutional, Cultural and Market Challenges
(b) Higher Education as a Global Commodity
(c) Quality and Perceptual Issues
(d) Challenges in Teaching, Administration and Research

2.15 Country, Institutional, Cultural and Market Challenges

Local environmental conditions will often be very different to those existing at the home campus (Lane, 2011a). Lane cites two examples highlighting specific country challenges. The recruitment of academic staff will be dependent upon country specific legalisation. For example, in the UAE, according to the UAE labour law, visas are only issued every three years. These are dependent on the renewal of an academic contract by the University and also passing stringent health conditions. For the expatriate academic, this poses uncertainty for long-term career prospects and undue stress. In Lane's second example, all Universities are faced with problems in the recruitment of students, as they tend to join very late prior to the start of the new semester. This has serious challenges for staff timetabling and operational planning in contrast to the UK UCAS system that is front-end loaded. Lane (2011a) also describes one case in which he investigated and found that all admissions files went back to the home campus for application consideration causing student frustration, as they had to await a decision from the local institution. The UAE student community want their decisions immediately. Austin and Chapman (2002) observe, "The history of educational development is littered with good ideas that failed, not because they lacked merit, but because their implementation overlooked important cultural and contextual factors that limited their success" (p. 254). Austin and Chapman argue that a systems approach is necessary to grasp the complexities and challenges facing Universities setting up overseas. Universities need to carefully analyse the country specific environment issues (political, economic and social) and how they will impact on themselves. According to Lane (2011a), "Academic leaders seem to make decisions based on extrapolations of knowledge about home institution environment without fully investigating host country environmental conditions" (p.368). Lane (2011a) refers to Michigan State University that had to withdraw its operation in Dubai International Academic City losing millions of dollars in 2009. The key reason for its failure was that it did not undertake proper market research and inaccurately over-estimated student demand based on a high student programme fee, which the market failed to respond to. Their student numbers after two years of operation reached only 80 students in total. Knight (2011) questions the sustainability of higher education hubs given the intense competition amongst Universities recruiting the same student base. She argues that there is very limited research to-date on the development and sustainability of overseas campuses and institutions, which identifies a gap in the current literature.

De Meyer (2012) suggests in his research (based upon the INSEAD Singapore campus) that there are particular problems associated with establishing an international overseas operation. Often senior management are very familiar and accustomed with their home campus operations but have limited experience and knowledge of international marketing, entry strategies or working in a multi-cultural environment. He argues in his discussion that there are five key challenges facing Universities in establishing and maintaining overseas operations. Firstly, he points out that it is extremely difficult to build and maintain a University brand. He uses the Middle East as an example where there is intense competition (similar to Knight 2011 and Lane 2011a) but takes this view further by suggesting that cost cutting actually has the opposite effect in depleting the brand. Wilkins (2010) undertook a survey of UAE institutes and highlighted the problem relating to oversupply and intense competition particularly in Business and Management programmes. Several of the UAE institutes have opted to turn towards recruiting overseas students to address this issue. He too agrees with De Meyer in that those Universities that are based in the UAE face problems in maintaining quality to stay competitive. Secondly, De Meyer (2012) suggests that the internationalisation of the academe is a challenge in itself. To be a successful institution, all academic staff must engage in global research and teaching. He observes that many overseas institutions fail to do so. This is also the viewpoint taken by Chapman and Austin (2002) who argue that greater attention should be addressed to the recruitment, training and support for the academe overseas. Austin and Chapman (2002) provides the example of academic staff working in South Africa who received very limited training on adapting teaching pedagogy or undertaking leadership roles overseas. Similar to Lane's (2011a) research, De Meyer suggests in his third point that Universities need to develop an effective business model but so often they rush into setting up the overseas operation without much due attention for the implications. De Meyer (2012) suggests fourthly that the leadership of overseas operations is often lacking in operating overseas campuses. Finally, he stresses the importance of technology in supporting globalisation of the University operations. De Meyer uses his own operation based at INSEAD (Singapore) in which they have invested heavily on video conferencing facilities which has brought about effective and enhanced communication links between their French and Singaporean counterparts.

There is a perception that overseas private higher education providers are not fully embracing quality assurance and enhancement. Part of the reason for this perception is that private sector universities and colleges are motivated by profit and are less likely to invest in resources and facilities compared to the home campuses (Lim, 2010). Naidoo (2007) posits that Universities tend to focus on overseas operations by building on "scale" rather than quality and that the strategy is often to produce standardised programmes (p. 20). In addition, overseas campuses often concentrate on programmes that are easier to teach (such as business) and require fewer resources. Programmes such as medicine, engineering and the sciences, which are essential for building economies and creating wealth in overseas countries are not normally delivered but yet exist in the home campus (Naidoo, 2007). McBurnie (2000) wrote on the development of Monash University as a case study and argued that library and teaching resources were under-resourced in many overseas campuses. Woodhouse and Stella (2008) examined fifteen overseas institutions and found similar under-funding in library and IT support and facilities. Limited research was also being undertaken, as the providers were mainly 'for profit' HE providers. A recent Quality Assurance Agency Overseas Transnational Review undertaken in the UAE in 2014 examining the quality of British Universities revealed that the lack of student support systems (such as careers and counselling), library and limited teaching accommodation did not allow British Universities to call themselves an International Branch Campuses (QAA, 2014). The QAA recognise that the comparison between host and home campuses is not the same in terms of the level of resourcing and infrastructure. This was also similar to the QAA's Overseas Review findings in China (QAA, 2012). This section is important to my study, as the research caters answers to find out how lower resources at overseas campuses impacts and affects the professional role of the expatriate academic.

Lane (2011b) suggests that time zone difference presents temporal boundaries in communicating between the host and home campus. For example, in the UAE, Universities teach between Sundays through to Thursday. Given the time differences and the reduction in the number of available days to communicate, this poses several challenges for meetings and dialogue between both campuses. Distance adds another layer of complexity in the relationship between the home and overseas campus. The relationship with the home campus is often seen as having a major impact on the academe working in overseas institutions. This area was investigated by Smith (2009) in her study at an overseas Australian campus (University of Wollongong Dubai) where the relationship was perceived as the "parent" versus the "child" institution that caused a certain amount of resentment at the offshore campus. "Relations were often strained and there seems to have been a series of miscommunications between the two campuses" (p. 472). When the University of Wollongong Dubai Campus transferred its accreditation to the Ministry of Higher Education, the control moved from the main campus to the Ministry impacting the relations between the two campuses. Smith (2009) posits, "The relationship with the home campus is seen as paramount in determining the quality of academic life" (p.477). Heffernan and Poole (2004) have identified four key determinants for a successful relationship to exist between the host and home campus-building trust, working on communication, developing commitment and respecting the cultural aspects of each institution. Dobos (2011) also found in her study of academics working at a Malaysian branch campus that they felt themselves as 'unequal' to those academics working at the home campus. One of the interviewees responded, "We have a master-slave relationship which is not good" (p.27). Dobos (2011) suggests that this can lead to poor morale and can cause academics to leave the overseas campus. Hughes (2011) also suggests that distance is a challenge and it is important to maintain and develop relationships between both parties. She also builds on this idea and suggests that 'expectations' are a challenge. Understanding 'expectations' from the different stakeholders (government, home and host campuses) and the extent and clarity of their autonomy can often avoid misunderstandings. Hughes (2011) was involved in the University of Nottingham (Ningbo campus based in China) for several years and describes her experience of establishing the branch campus as a 'belt and braces' approach to managing staff at the growth stage (p.20). She argues in her research study that staff values are a challenge for those employed in an overseas environment. Academic staff come from many different countries with variations of education systems and it may often be difficult to manage the expectations of the values required and those expected by the UK home campus. Hughes (2011) also raises the argument that integration and respect for academic staff is a challenge – to what extent does the home campus listen to overseas-based staff? This is an important point as it links closely to the fundamental core principle (respect) put forward by Gappa et al (2007) in their "Framework of Core Essential Elements" explained later in Part Three. It is also important as a key area to understand in this study how distance and communication between campuses affect the professional role of the expatriate academic.

Hughes (2011) also argues that there is often tension of academic career expectations and what the overseas campus provides – "these issues may be around career progression, salary, terms and conditions (e.g. maternity or sick pay), professional development opportunities and so on. This is almost inevitable in any employee-employer situation, but the branch campus environment and the nature of university teaching can exacerbate the situation" (p. 26). Hughes (2011) puts forward the point that as an overseas campus matures, this issue will become clearer. Nevertheless, the research by Hughes raises many fundamental questions as to the comparability of academic work between the home and host campuses. In her conclusion, she refers to the research conducted by McBurnie and Ziguras (2007) who argue: "too many accounts of teaching in transnational programs begin with an unquestioned view of academic life, in which tenured staff engages in a life's work of research, teaching and community service within a community of scholars. Invariably, the conditions of work in branch campus or local partner institutions fall far short of the ideal for most commentators, and conclusions generally revolve around the question of how to make academic work in these peripheries more like the traditional ideal" (p.50). The study by Hughes (2011) raises several questions about career progression for expatriate academics and how their international experience is perceived in the UK if they are to return back to the UK HE sector. Another area that is not well covered in the literature is how the professional role of the expatriate academic differs to the UK HE academic?

The literature indicates that there is often lack of preparation provided to academics on pre-departure training for developing cultural skills and knowledge on the country as well as teaching in a new country. These studies suggest widespread challenges faced by expatriate academics. One of the key reasons for taking up academic posts overseas has revealed that seeking 'an adventure' and opportunities for travel as the most dominant reason (Thorn, 2009; Richardson, 2000). According to Richardson and McKenna (2002), "the expatriate academic can be seen as an explorer in that taking an overseas position presented an opportunity both to explore another culture and to undertake this exploration in an independent way through living and learning in a new culture" (p.70). The study was undertaken with thirty UK expatriate academics working it the UAE, Turkey, New Zealand

and Singapore. Several of the interviewees responded that they were also 'escaping' the UK HE system due to the challenges and changes that had taken place in the UK HE sector. Others suggested that they were using their overseas experience, as it would be useful in returning home to build an international curriculum, teaching international students and international research collaboration. In their research study, many interviewees spoke of their challenges when arriving, often last minute in teaching preparation, difficulties facing students in teaching first-time (or previously overseas), setting up home, personal challenges such as integrating with locals or settling in the family to the new environment.

Another area investigated was that of returning home. Many expatriate academics suggested that there was always a risk of losing their jobs due to the short-term contracts (one or three years) dependent on the country with no job to go back to. All respondents stated that they had experienced personal change in their lives and grown in personal and professional development since taking up employment overseas. This is similar to the Schermerhorn's (1999) personal account of working at a Malaysian campus where he stated that the experiences made him more productive in his future working environments. Schermerhorn (1999) reveals that his family went through a period of two years of cultural adjustment. They faced "a period of initial enthusiasm followed by some disillusionment and finally a time of adaptation and accommodation" (p.253). He accounts that he did not receive a package which multinational companies normally provide to staff. Napier (1997) worked and provided a personal account of setting up a business school in Vietnam. He too accounts that academic staff faced challenges in working and teaching. They had to adapt to cultural issues both inside and outside the classroom.

In all three studies there is a common theme emerging of 'culture shock'. Oberg (1960) suggests that this can lead to a number of negative outcomes – stress; depression; confusion; a sense of loss resulting from loss of friends, personal possessions, status and roles; fear of being rejected; confusion in cultural adjustment and variation. Pyvis and Chapman (2005) suggest that this area is an important issue considering that both academics and students are involved in such a scale of overseas operations. According to Ward et al (2001), difficulties for expatriates exist "because they are mostly left to sink or swim on their own" (p.16). The authors explain that in the business sector this is often common. Pre-departure training is deemed elementary and non-effective. They posit, "the challenge, therefore, is to understand and manage contact between culturally diverse people and groups in order to reduce the stresses and difficulties that are a normal aspect of such encounters" (p.18). Cultural understanding can often occur by understanding people's gestures, eye contact and address for example. "For instance, Arabs tend to speak loudly which Europeans interpret as shouting" (Ward et al, 2001, p.55). Jochems et al (1996) conducted a research study of the intercultural classroom and found that international students perceive language ability as the greatest challenge affecting academic performance followed by learning styles and cultural adjustment in the classroom. A study by Teekens (2003) into teaching in a multi-cultural setting found that academics do not reflect on their current teaching practices and tended to teach how they learnt in their own society where they studied themselves. Ward et al (2001) provide two examples where this applies. "From one perspective, quiet but attentive collectivist students may be perceived as uninterested or withdrawn by individualist teachers. From another viewpoint, the relatively frequent interruptions to lectures by individualist students may be seen as rude and unmannered by their collectivist classmates" (p.157). Ward et al (2001) posit that the vast majority of expatriates receive limited effective inter-cultural training that could greatly benefit their work performance through behavioural changes. One of the reasons why this does not happen is due to the high expense of training firms and consultants in this area of expertise. Gopal (2011) also suggests that shortage of time; priority or resource could be factors into why expatriate academics do not receive intercultural training. The implications for transnational higher education institutions is that it will affect the expatriate academic and have a negative impact on the quality of the overall student learning experience. Intercultural learning is a major feature of internationalisation. Leask (2004) argues that if academics find it difficult to teach international students at home, how can they teach students overseas? He argues that teaching overseas is an emotional journey.

Given the current literature it would be useful to examine in this study if motives to move overseas have changed over the 15-year period as informed by Richardson (2000). In addition, have the problems in settling-in and lack of induction been solved? Are these challenges different or similar to the UAE HE sector?

2.16 Higher Education as a Global Commodity

A major theme that emerges from the International Higher Education literature is that of 'commodification' and its ramifications for the academic who teaches in overseas institutions. 'Commodification' is essentially a curriculum that is re-produced by home campus academics and delivered identically in the overseas branch/institution. More often, the 'commoditised' curriculum is delivered overseas without the same facilities and resources that exist at the home campus. Naidoo (2007) strongly argues that "commoditised systems tend to be lean systems which strip away all these elements which are not strictly necessary, there is likely to be little or no investment in facilities such as libraries or social facilities which promote peer-based interaction" (p.8). According to Schapper and Mayson (2004), they posit that introducing a standardised curriculum overseas is a "Taylorist assault on the professionalism of academic staff" (p. 189). This is an important fundamental aspect of International Higher Education as it restricts the academic in his/her own research-led teaching where many researchers suggest the need to localise and contextualise. Research by Clarke (2013) at a UAE based IBC indicated the difficulty in using other's teaching materials if they had not created it themselves. Some interviewees expressed that there were several instances where the teaching materials were completely not relevant to the country context. For example, one interviewee stated that his course content (created by the home campus) referred to the application of UK central heating systems whereas the UAE used entirely air conditioning systems. Schapper and Mayson (2004) argue that teaching a "commoditised" curriculum actually strips the autonomy of the academic and is what the authors "feel to be the greatest attack on contemporary academic work today" (p.195). The engineer, Frederick Taylor who was pursuing productivity and efficiency gains in the workplace, based his work upon the theory of scientific management. Introducing standardised tools, procedures and systems meant that managers assumed greater control over workers. Schapper and Mayson argue that web based technology has helped to establish the 'tools' and enable the standardisation of the curriculum to be implemented. Schapper and Mayson (2004) argue "academic teaching staff in this context is no longer valued for their intellectual contribution to student learning but their ability to deliver pre-packaged education with efficiency and economy" (p.197). They argue that this impinges on intellectual freedom which Allport (2000) describes as "the rights of academic staff to freely discuss, teach, assess, develop curricula, publish and research and engage in community service" (p.43). It is view of Schapper and Mayson (2004) that teaching a commoditised curriculum 'robs' the academic of intellectual stimulation and engagement, judgement and professional autonomy (p.198).

Schoorman (2000b) posits that 'conceptualisation' (theory that can be adapted to country specific examples) can be useful in developing a more creative approach to curriculum development and assessment. For Schoorman (2000b), this means adopting variations to accommodate for multiple country perspectives. It can also lead to regaining some of the ground lost in autonomy and professional judgement for the overseas academics. In short, ownership of the curriculum reverts back to the academic. In addition, the researcher argues that this should also be embraced for teaching pedagogy. She encourages and supports a student-centred approach to learning and teaching that is unbiased to one particular culture and is not likely therefore to privilege one culture over another culture.

Schapper and Mayson (2004) suggest that Universities should embrace the guidelines of Whalley (1997) for developing an international curriculum and learning for students. These guidelines encourage critical thinking, independent learning and self-reflection, problem-solving skills, University participation and a detailed examination of both intercultural and global perspectives (p. 201). Whalley (1997) encourages applying the use of international case studies, global issues, diversity and ethics. Both Schapper and Mayson (2004) argue in their research study that the adoption of Whalley's guidelines and

Schoorman's suggestions require considerable resources to address the effect of "Taylorism". Woodhouse and Stella (2008) examined offshore institutions and found that contextualisation of the curriculum to local examples was seen as positive. However, academics were still challenged in adapting to local teaching pedagogy that adjusted to local needs of students. Hughes (2011) also confers with this finding stating in her involvement with Nottingham University's Ningbo campus that learning and teaching styles conflict with the needs of the student body. She cites, "problems will emerge where the aspirations of the wider institution and the activities of the IBC are not in harmony, or where the institutional philosophy or strategies are not aligned to the needs of the IBC students and the surrounding society. An example of the former would be teaching staff who prefer to teach to the textbook and test facts when the institution is aiming to provide a more autonomous and critical teaching and learning environment for its students" (p.23). Hughes (2011) also suggests that there needs to be extensive debate on how the local market can be catered for to adjust the curriculum.

For globalised Universities, there are indeed many attractions to commodification as it leads to standardised curricula, assessment, consistency of approach between campuses and efficiencies if both campuses use one set of materials (Schapper and Mayson, 2004). The technologies used to assist the development and growth of transnational higher education is influencing higher staff: student ratios (p.198).

Schoorman's (2000b) principle of contextualisation has not been fully implemented globally. A major study conducted by Mahrous and Ahmed (2010) of 461 undergraduate students located in the Middle East, UK and USA investigated students' perceptions of the effectiveness of pedagogical tools on programme performance. Their findings revealed significant differences in learning styles between Western and Middle East countries. For example, there is a strong reliance (in the Middle East) on examinations where memorisation (rote learning and recall) of facts is employed by students. This method had been adopted previously in the student schooling education systems. This contrasts to western education, which places greater empathis on "interactive education", and exams/assignments that apply course concepts (p.291). At school, students in the Middle East education system focus on the individual and do not participate in group work activities. Communication and teamwork is neither utilised nor developed. According to Smith (2006), cited in Mahrous and Ahmed (2010, p.293), "the pedagogical tools and approaches proven to be effective in Western countries may not be very effective in Middle East countries." In addition, Mahrous and Ahmed found that case studies and computerised simulation games proved difficult for Middle East students as they had a passive learning style and found it challenging to develop decision modelling in this 'new' learning mode. They also did not normally read peer reviewed articles but did excel at Multiple Choice Question tests. The studies by Dobos (2011) and Clarke (2013) also confirm that the challenges in developing effective learning styles strategies have not been fully addressed. Naidoo (2007) is critical that transnational higher education is delivered without the involvement of 'deep processing' which is essential for producing high quality graduates (p.9). Graduates from these Universities may not be able to adapt to their own country labour market. Yet, she argues that this is essential "for capacity building in developing countries" (p.10). Naidoo (2003) argues that a commoditised curriculum narrows down the students' ability to learn and adapt to a changing world and suggests that it leads to declining quality in overseas higher education.

The commodification of the curriculum also reflects the explicit and 'hidden' curriculum strategies of western Universities (Naidoo, 2011, p.12). Naidoo (2011) suggests that Western academics influence transnational higher education through their attitudes and behaviours whilst the nature of the curriculum (such as the creation of employability skills embedded into the UK curriculum discussed in Part One) is directly transported as a package abroad in overseas campuses. Miller-Idriss and Hanauer (2011) are also of the view that expatriate academics impose "cultural imperialism" as they adopt their cultures into classrooms from their home countries. Woolf (2002) argues that an international curriculum is extremely difficult to standardise as "the education system of any given country is necessarily shaped by the culture of that country" (p.9). He argues that educationalists should focus on the understanding of cultural diversity. He cites the example where American students prefer debate in the classroom and the professor playing the role of 'devil's advocate'. In Eastern society, they would find this difficult to accept. In an Eastern society, students recognise that the professor as someone who has "unchallenged wisdom" (p.12). Robson (2001) reviewed the literature on internationalisation and found that many researchers argued that the curriculum projected colonisation with both content and assessment that are 'western' focused and do not address specific cultural needs. In terms of internationalisation, she suggests that issues will arise if the academic community is not fully involved particularly with regarding teaching pedagogy and intercultural relations. Robson (2001) suggests that further research be undertaken to explore student assessment that would help both students and academics alike in developing an international approach. Coryell et al (2012) reviewed four Universities on internationalisation and found that there was a need for the entire staff to "develop and acquire intercommunication skills, knowledge of international practices in one's discipline, and transcultural sensitivity" (p.90). Their findings revealed the lack of evaluation in assessing student learning and experiences in conjunction with the main University and its role in internationalisation. Thus, there is a strong need in all cases to adopt a shared approach amongst all academics and administrative staff.

The area of standardisation versus conceptualisation versus complete adaptation of the curriculum (tailored to the specific country needs) clearly reflects a debate in how home campuses deliver their degree programmes overseas. How it affects the professional role of the expatriate opens up an interesting question that needs to be investigated from this research study.

2.17 Quality and Perceptual Issues

The rapid expansion of transnational higher education in the past two decades has raised concerns amongst the academic community over the quality of its provision (Altbach and Knight, 2006). One factor that contributes to this concern is that academics face challenges in teaching international students at home-based Universities. For example, Crossman and Burdett (2012) conducted a large-scale study examining fourteen Australian Universities on the academic performance of the international students compared to home students. Their findings highlighted that international students do not perform as well academically compared to home based students. In addition, language and learning styles proved difficult for these students. Given this evidence, the authors suggest similar (if not worse results) reflected of the academic performance of students located in a transnational higher education setting. Distance often leads to tensions and the perception of a lowering of academic standards (Hughes, 2011). Harding and Lammey (2011) argue that distance between the host and home campuses can often lead to an 'oversight' of the operation and can be a potential risk to the reputation of the University. They suggest developing coordination and effective working relationships, as they are important key factors to making the partnership work effectively. Hughes (2011) argues that home staff need to listen to what local staff have to say and contribute. Her research study revealed that stakeholder expectations on autonomy can often lead to misunderstandings and this could be reduced/eliminated if properly planned and developed from the outset. Research by Dunworth (2008) also suggests that developing goodwill and respect helps improve academic standards but also points out the significance of shared values and principles between parties. Heffernan and Poole (2004) also argue the latter point of view.

There are very few studies that help to address working relationships and trust between virtual teams (i.e. host staff communicating with home campus staff). Few studies have ever been conducted into this field. Panteli and Tucker (2009) examined the successful factors that lead to effective and productive virtual teams in a global IT company. They suggest that problems arise due to time differences and little or no social interest between individual/groups and recommend three solutions. Firstly, they suggest that parties should meet face to face wherever possible. Heffernan and Poole (2004) also raised this point, which examined successful working relationships between the host and home campuses as it helps, secures trust and commitment. Secondly, they recommend regular computer mediated communication (i.e. Skype). Thirdly, they recommend that all parties work and develop social interaction. Such factors were found in effective working partnerships. As discussed earlier in Smith's (2009) study on an Australian campus in Dubai that the relationship ('parent' versus 'child' relationship) has a major influence on the effect of the academic's work. "The relationship with the home campus is seen as paramount in determining the quality of academic life" (Smith, 2009, p.477). It can be a contributing factor that reduces stress for both academics and administrators alike. In the Dobos (2011) study of a Malaysian campus, the academics felt themselves as 'unequal'. Dobos (2011) describes this as leading to a loss of morale amongst the academics working at the host campus. Academic staff claimed that assessments and teaching materials were sent out late by the home University staff causing them frustration and stress. The relationship not only has an effect upon academics but also can determine the overall association between the quality of programmes. Heffernan and Poole (2004) saw a direct linkage between relationship and quality by examining eleven Australian overseas transnational country review reports in their literature review. They posit, "despite such obvious indicators of success, there appears to be concern across the university sector for the quality of many partnerships, for the on-going strength of existing partnerships, and for the sustainability of offshore education relationships as they are established and developed across nations, cultures and industries" (p.77). Dobos (2011) concludes that academics need to be treated professionally by home campus staff for the overseas campus to be successful.

Castle and Kelly (2010) examined the literature on quality assurance over the past two decades. They found that up until 1999, there was very limited research or literature available on the quality of transnational higher education. The gap has since closed but is still haphazard. They conclude that the vast majority of the literature indicates that overseas providers are adopting a standardised curriculum although the authors suggest that this is derisive against quality. Common themes emerge such as a varying student learning styles, poor teaching resources and facilities, cultural sensitivity issues and differences to the home campus are major challenges raising issues in ensuring quality assurance. Coleman (2003) describes the quality assurance of transnational higher education in its infancy and that transnational higher education is the least monitored in all Higher Education domains. He concludes that there are real differences between the home and host campus in terms of academic performance resulting from lower resources and academic staff qualifications. His research involved eighty-eight interviews with both staff and students at two branch campuses located in Malaysia and Indonesia. Students in both countries found it difficult to adapt to critical thinking approaches. He also found 'drift' creeping in particularly with adapting the curriculum despite employing a shared curricula and assessment strategy. Coleman (2003) noted that the Australian Universities Quality Agency (AUQA) had conducted eight institutional audits, five of which had insufficient quality assurance mechanisms in place. Then, no performance indicators between the home and host campuses were analysed. Coleman writes, "at this stage, it is simply not known with certainty whether students in the huge number of offshore programs receive the same educational experience as those in traditional campus structures" (p.373).

Chapman and Austin (2002) suggest that whilst governments place quality at the top of their agendas, universities strive for 'efficiency' that in turn leads to 'resistance' to government goals. They posit, "absorbing more students requires resources that might otherwise be spent on quality" (p.257). They also purport that the recruitment, training and support of academic staff and academic leaders is fundamental to ensuring and improving quality assurance.

Cheung (2006) suggests that transnational higher education has more advantages than disadvantages. However, he argues that there are many 'second-rate' providers operating overseas and that governments should do more to identify good providers that match industry requirements. In this way, quality will be a key driver to moving forward the globalisation of higher education. The research conducted by Chapman and Pyvis (2006) indicates that students' quality of life is positively correlated with their course evaluations at overseas campuses. This has implications for transnational providers, as they must become more client focused. "The finding suggest that the quality of the overall learning experience of students engages in off-shore education by a sense of belonging to the learning community" (p.241).

A major study by Austin and Chapman (2002) examining quality assurance of fifteen Australian overseas institutions revealed the need for greater accountability in the roles of the Academic Board and their transnational campuses. There were often missing procedures and frameworks for monitoring the provision that was deemed as an oversight. Their study revealed that overseas campuses depended greatly on the use of part-time academics, which had a negative effect on the student learning experience. The researchers found that induction and lack of cultural awareness training was detrimental to quality. They noted that there were many cases where low English language entry standards caused poor academic performance. In addition, limited library facilities and IT support were observed at these overseas campuses. Academic staff conducted no research, as the providers were 'for profit'. When examining comparability in programme progression rates, the home campus performed much better compared to all overseas campuses. Austin and Chapman (2002) suggest that there is a dilemma in expanding transnational higher education whilst achieving quality and obtaining academic standards. The rapid growth has therefore serious implications for pedagogy practices and the development of the academic community.

Various stakeholders often perceive quality differently (e.g. government, host campus and home campus). According to Lim (2010), "they may disagree regarding how to measure quality and what to measure to determine quality. The result is the development of different mechanisms based on what each stakeholder deems appropriate, leading to several challenges in the management of transnational higher education" (p.212). Smith (2010) examined the discourse used in the documentation of USA, Australian and UK Quality Assurance systems and argued that the wording presented in the documentation can often lead to misrepresentation by the various stakeholders. The author used critical discourse to analyse the quality assurance documentation. Smith (2010) found that in all three countries, there was the opportunity to adapt courses to meet local market needs. "In the UK code, however, warnings against localisation and the implied lack of confidence in the abilities of the partner institution seen to militate against real adaption" (p.803). Smith (2010) purports that both home and host academics should work together to achieve a globalised curricula which allows for local relevance (p.804).

Pyvis (2011) studied a Chinese institution, which was a franchise of an Australian University. The Chinese institution adopted identical quality and standards to that of the home campus. The author found this to be problematic in applying "educational imperialism and that guidelines and practices should be altered to embrace context-sensitive measures of quality" (p.733). Pyvis (2011) agrees with De La Feunte who has suggested that quality should be multiple rather than one-sided given the diverse needs of stakeholders (De la Feunte is the President of the International Association of Universities speaking at the 2010 Bologna forum). Given the distance and cultural sensitivity, this has proved to be of great difficulty in achieving and he found that relationships between the host and home campus was essential and that goodwill was often required. When staff members left (on either side) this affected the overall quality of programmes. "As is apparent from this example, using a home programme as the reference point for quality and striving for 'sameness' encourages educational imperialism not educational diversity" (p.741). Pyvis (2011) argues that it is improper for educators to apply 'sameness' in transnational higher education. He argues that 'sameness' is identified to 'comparable' although the Guidelines for Quality in the Provision of Cross-Border Higher Education (produced by UNESCO/OECD 2005) state that the programmes should be of 'comparable' quality (p.743). Pyvis argues that context sensitive measures of quality could be a more effective way to deliver in a global higher education market.

Relationships and communications between expatriate academics and their counter-parts play a vital role in improving perception and building trust between parties. Studies have shown how this affects the relationship between the host and home campus can have a negative impact on quality. The theme of communication between campuses is an important area that will be investigated in this research study given the dearth of literature available. In particular, it will examine how it affects the role of the expatriate academic.

2.18 Teaching, Research and Administration

While there is abundant literature on the issues and challenges affecting overseas campuses, there are limited research studies on the academics that work in a transnational higher education setting. Fielden and Gillard (2011) conducted a large research study involving nine case studies located overseas investigating staffing strategies. The authors purport that it is very difficult to create a research culture in the early stages of a branch campus. It tends to emerge much later when the operation is well established and mature. They cite one case, the University of Wollongong Dubai campus, "UOWD has also a strong research ethos, but Wollongong describes it as 'an overnight success that took 17 years', which should be a caution about the time required to develop a research profile locally" (p.31). Research at 'with-profit' institutions is often viewed by management as an unnecessary expense. In addition, it is often extremely difficult to obtain research funding from government bodies. As Chapman et al (2014) UAE study reveals that often "it is an expectation, but an afterthought" (p.148). Given the heavy teaching loads reported (70-80% of their time), there is limited available time to conduct research work. Fielden and Gillard's study make a general point on those academics choosing a career abroad – "they have often chosen an expatriate life and in some cases abandoned hopes of active research careers" (p.22). They also found that few British academics are willing to locate to overseas campuses as they see this as a threat to their career opportunities.

Salt and Wood (2014) investigated four Universities who were involved in operating transnational HE provision. In their study, one of the Pro Vice Chancellors is quoted as saying, "If we were to do it again it would be interesting to see if we could persuade people to go out in the early stages of their careers to set up because the most (currently) research active people tend not to want to do something like that" (p. 90). They also found that academics that did limited research were more willing to travel abroad. One Pro Vice Chancellor is quoted as saying, "You do find there is a group of staff that perhaps are not cutting it research wise that are good teachers and also good citizens and they are willing to go" (p.91). Salt and Wood (2014) found that many teaching staff that work in overseas campuses have tended to be recruited from outside the UK. They suggest that it is important for Universities who are involved in overseas operations "to address a central dilemma in transmitting their home-based "institutional DNA" abroad" (p.94).

Clarke (2013) examined the challenges faced by expatriate academics at an International Branch Campus based in Dubai and found frustration from the respondents on the level of research undertaken. One of the interviewees is cited as saying, "this is a problem I am facing – I am frustrated that it will affect my career life. I want to be both a researcher and a teacher" (Clarke, 2013, p.24). Clarke (2013) identified four reasons for limited research being undertaken. Firstly, there are limited government grants available in the UAE. Secondly, there is no research community base in providing the momentum required. Thirdly, there are few conferences or research series in the region. Fourthly, the branch is detached from the home campus and distance prevents support and collaboration from the home campus staff.

The Fielden and Gillard (2011) study revealed that academics raised concerns over the amount of administrative tasks that they had to undertake overseas in contrast to their UK peers. Part of the reason for this was that the administration function of the overseas campus was either under-resourced or lacked the skills or knowledge of counterparts in the UK. In Clarke's (2013) study, he found that academic staff performed additional administration duties compared to their colleagues at the UK campus. These duties involved a large amount of marketing activity, dealing with admission applications, timetabling and following up on student queries.

Academics working abroad face numerous challenges in their teaching pedagogy which stems from both cultural misunderstandings and language barriers (Hofstede 1986; Napier et al 1997; Welch 1998; Bodycott and Walker 2000; Richardson 2000; Chapman and Austin 2002; Woolf 2002; Teekens 2003; Richardson and McKenna 2003; Smith 2009; Sulkowski and Deakin 2009; Montgomery 2009; Tan 2010; Zhang and Mi 2010; Nieto and Booth 2010; Hamza 2010; Crose 2011; Caluya et al 2011; Lane 2011a; Selmer and Lauring 2011; Miller-Idriss and Hanauer 2011; De Meyer 2012; Clarke 2013). There is common agreement that teaching abroad is both challenging and demanding. Studies by Leask (2004) and Dunn and Wallace (2006) found that there is a clear difference in teaching international students in the home campus compared to teaching overseas students. Expatriate academics had to deal with perception differences that are challenging. Given the limited support or training before taking up a position overseas, on arrival and in post this has been a major issue for the expatriate academic. Clarke (2013) identified this as the greatest academic issue when he investigated the priority of the challenges faced by academics at a large British Branch Campus based in the United Arab Emirates. One of the interviewees stated that she lost her hair due to stress in coping with the new teaching environment. Several interviewees suggested that they developed stress as they were unfamiliar with new courses and this required more time on top of their heavy teaching loads. One interviewee compared his experiences of teaching Asian students at an Australian branch campus in Dubai and found that the Dubai students tended to be less mature and not motivated to learn. It meant that teaching staff had to be stricter in this teaching environment. All academics commented on that the lack of country specific examples and case studies were often difficult to find particularly at the start of taking up their position. Several academics suggested the need to build in more skills for overseas students to cope with the UK degree programmes. One academic is quoted as saying, "You have to entertain them in shorter class intervals as their attention span is short" (Clarke, 2013, p.23). Another is cited as saying, "It is a different type of student coming to the Dubai Campus yet they are treated on the same par with the home campus – we disadvantage the students as their learning styles are completely different to Edinburgh" (Clarke, 2013, p.20). All interviewees in Clarke's study responded that stress was attached to teaching in this multi-cultural environment and all found it difficult to adjust their teaching styles to the various multi-cultural students who attended the lectures and tutorials. Despite many of the academics participating or having completed the University's Postgraduate Certificate in Teaching practice programme, this did not cover teaching to multi-cultural students. Many academics in Clarke's study found that students approached academics outside normal class timings or office hours which meant a lot of interruptions and frustration when it came to marking, preparing for class or the tranquillity necessary to undertake effective scholarly activity.

Teaching multi-cultural groups presents challenges for academics in "overcoming psychological problems" associated with students who come from a variety of cultures and with differing sets of language skills (Gabb, 2006, p.357). Gabb (2006) argues that teaching involves managing the class socio-cultural dynamics and this is not often performed well by academics in the classroom and they often develop stress as a result (similar to Bodycott and Walker, 2000). Gabb (2006) suggests several teaching strategies to support academics teaching overseas students in a multi-cultural setting. She stresses that teachers should avoid using any slang or metaphors as it confuses students. Clear explanation should always be used in class. She suggests that the first lesson of a class should focus on getting to know one another and how the subject area translates into cultural themes and settings. Examples or cases used in class should always relate to other student cultures.

Bodycott and Walker (2000) taught at an overseas institution based in Hong Kong. Their research examined the challenges facing academics who taught abroad – they both faced stress and alienation when arriving to the country and recount their experiences of bringing their own values and beliefs into the classroom. They argue that having a positive and enquiring attitude is fundamental to developing new cross-cultural awareness and understanding in the classroom. They describe how Hong Kong students did not like to "lose face" and one of their teaching strategies employed was to break the students down into smaller groups where they would develop group opinion and debate. The authors found that the students liked to share their direct experiences as the stimulus for class discussion.

2.18.1 Contribution by Geert Hofstede

Geert Hofstede is a leading social psychologist who undertook a pioneering study of cultures across the world in the late 1970s and early 1980s. His work is particularly important to the understanding of overseas teaching and learning and to this study. According to Hofstede (1986), academics must adopt their cross-cultural teaching and learning when they teach overseas. He suggests that problems occur in overseas teaching environments from four main circumstances. Firstly, differences can occur in the social position of the teacher and the position of those students studying in the host country. Hofstede (1986) provides an example of the Chinese teacher as being highly respected. Secondly, he suggests that differences may occur in the relevance of the curriculum applied between the host and home campus. Hofstede uses the example of an Organisational Behaviour course being replicated by a British lecturer in China. "There are strong forces that perpetuated the transfer of irrelevant knowledge" (Hofstede, 1986, p.304). Thirdly, differences often occur in cognitive abilities that exist between the teacher and students or to the student populations existing in each society. Hofstede purports that cognitive development is determined largely upon individual upbringing and are influenced by one's society. As Hofstede (1986) cites, "teaching to a student or student body with a cognitive ability profile different from what the teacher is accustomed to is evidently problematic. It demands a different didactic approach, for which the teacher may lack the cognitive abilities" (p. 305). Fourthly, there may be differences in the interaction between students or the teacher/student themselves (p.301/p.303). According to Hofstede (1986), roles tend to play out in cultural settings, "which means that cross-cultural learning situations are rife with premature judgements" (p.305). Hofstede developed the four-dimensional model of cultural differences which was based on his statistical analysis alongside his personal experience (whilst working at IMEDE and INSEAD) and interviewing participants attending the International Teachers programme who held extensive international teaching experience. Hofstede's Four Dimension Model (1986) is examined below:

2.18.1.1 Individualism versus Collectivism

Individualistic cultures primarily look after their own self-interests and their immediate family members. In contrast, collectivist cultures belong to tightly bound integrated communities (Hofstede, 1986). Using Hofstede's research, Great Britain is identified as an individualistic society. In a teaching and learning context, the student is expected to become skilled at how to learn and speak up in class catering impartiality from teachers. Hofstede (1986) stated in his research study, "education is a way of improving one's economic worth and self-respect based on ability and competence" (p.312). In collectivist societies, formalised behaviour is practiced in the classroom and individual students will only speak up in class when asked to do so by the teacher. He also asserted "education is a way of gaining prestige in one's social environment and of joining a higher status group" (p.312). South Korea is an example of a collectivist society.

2.18.1.2 Power Distance

This is a characteristic of a culture in which less powerful individuals accept inequality of power and consider it to be a normal practice (Hofstede, 1986). For example, high power difference is prevalent in countries such as the Arab world or India. Respect for the teacher is always shown both inside and outside the classroom. France is an example of a country that has low power distance. Students speak up spontaneously in class and can question or contradict the teacher. France is based upon a student-centred education system.

2.18.1.3 Uncertainty Avoidance

This is a characteristic of a culture that is uncomfortable with new or unpredictable situations and as a result maintains strict behavioural codes to embed order in society. According to Hofstede (1986), "cultures with a strong uncertainty avoidance are active, aggressive, emotional, compulsive, security-seeking and intolerant; cultures with a weak uncertainty avoidance are contemplative, less aggressive, unemotional, relaxed, accepting personal risks, and relatively tolerant" (p.308). In countries where weak uncertainty avoidance dominance exists (such as in Jamaica) students will be familiar and comfortable to settings with a lingering presence of unstructured learning. In contrast to this, in strong uncertainty avoidance societies (such as in the case of Japan) students feel comfortable in a controlled and structured learning situation where there are clear objectives and guidelines provided in class.

2.18.1.4 Masculine versus Femininity

According to Hofstede (1986), "in masculine cultures these political/organisation values stress material success and assertiveness; in feminine cultures they stress other types of quality of life, interpersonal relationships, and concern for the weak" (p.308). For example, Ireland is a masculine society. In Ireland, students will compete and make themselves visible with each other in the class. In a masculine society, it is noted that students will avoid feminine academic subjects such as nursing. The teachers openly praise students who have performed well and will use the best students as the norm. Contrast this to Chile, which is a feminine society, students will behave modestly and practice mutual solidarity. For the teacher in a feminine society, they will avoid openly praising their students and will use the average student as their norm.

The implications of Hofstede's research are that the teacher should understand his/her culture and teaching traits and should adapt to the societal needs of their students. Hofstede argues that the focus of the expatriate academic should be centred upon "learning about his/her culture: getting intellectually and emotionally accustomed to the fact that in other societies, people learn in different ways" (p.316).

Hofstede (1986) suggests that teachers should teach in the students' first language as opposed to learning in the language of the teacher's language as language is the essence of culture itself and the tutor can understand the sensitivity of the students' culture itself. Hofstede provides an example from personal experience in which he teaches the same course delivered in either English or French. The materials were translated into either language. He argued, "the conclusion is that what represents a "message" in one language does not necessarily survive as a message in the other language; and this process of loss of meaning works both ways. Information is more than words – it is words which fit in a cultural framework" (p.316). This is an important point that Hofstede makes in that it helps one to explain the difficulties that the expatriate faces in teaching students more than often in their second language. The research by Zhang and Mi (2010) confirm that poor academic skills were interconnected to a poor level in a second language. This is one of reasons why academic writing skills are becoming an essential component of learning and teaching strategy for international and overseas students.

Clarke (2013) identified three camps of thought on Hofstede's research into teaching, student learning and culture. In one camp, the "supporters" (those in agreement with Hofstede and share his findings to be similar), those "against" (who are in disagreement or have developed models which reflect more modern times) and those that are "in-between" the two camps (middle ground view). In reviewing the literature available, Clarke (2013) found that there was a trend and linkage between the "supporters" studies and the research undertaken whereby expatriate academics teach mainly to local nationals in their home country. For example, in the research study conducted by Eldridge and Cranston (2009), they researched managers operating at Thailand overseas campuses. They used Hofstede's cultural dimension framework as the conceptual framework and found that Thai students avoided critical debate although the Australian curriculum endorsed this practice. Both authors agreed with Hofstede and found the dimensions to be consistent with their research. Cultural differences in teaching and learning presented many challenges in teaching pedagogy, assessment procedures and the overall social interaction involved in the operation of programmes. Similar findings are repeated in Bodycott and Walker's (2000) experience of teaching in Hong Kong; to the Schermerhorn (1999) experience in a Malaysian campus and to Napier's (1997) establishment of a Business School in Vietnam.

Those researchers opposed to Hofstede's research find his work to be very limited in an educational context due to the inconsistencies and oversimplification in cultural differences (Signorini et al, 2009). They argue that Hofstede's data set was derived from IBM employees and this cannot be used in the context of learning and teaching. They also posit that for different Universities, just like in business organisations, organisational behaviour does not always reflect the culture of the nation. They claim that Hofstede's study is deemed to be out-dated (over thirty years ago) and does not reflect the forces of globalisation. A research study conducted by Sulkowski and Deakin (2009) found that Indian and Sri Lankan students tended to be relaxed with authority whereas Hofstede's study stated the opposite. Sulkowski and Deakin (2009) concluded that a common element of all cultures is that education motivates all students and that it is a worthwhile pursuit. Biggs (2003) argues that academics should not focus on culture but should focus upon student similarities. He is conclusive that the problem does not stem from the student themselves but from both the teacher and that of the institution. Sanderson (2008) suggests that being a 'cosmopolitan' academic allows reflection upon oneself to internationalise their personal and professional development. He opposes Hofstede view on "knowing a lot about other's cultures" and argues that being 'cosmopolitan' is someone who is open to other's cultures (p.276). He strongly argues that staff development training should avoid using a "hints and tips" approach and should focus on coaching which produces real attitudinal and behavioural changes (p.297).

In the 'middle' camp, Durkin (2008) undertook a four year study of forty-two East Asian students and found that these students rejected critical thinking which is applied in western educational systems and instead moved towards a middle ground which acquired "to sustain a more conciliatory approach that allows space for diversity of opinions" and which helped "to preserve the dignity and integrity of all students" (p.48). Durkin argues that such an approach avoids humiliating other cultures based in a multi-cultural classroom setting. Tan (2010) studied 1,000 Malaysian and Chinese adult learners who were undertaking professional development programmes. He suggests that rote learning is deeply embedded in the East Asian culture and takes many years to learn from childhood. Whilst he agrees with the findings of Hofstede, particularly on the societal aspect of learning and that it is difficult to impose another society's learning system onto students, he suggests that a combination of rote learning and understanding can actually improve one's learning ability.

The research undertaken by Hofstede (1986) is important to the understanding of student learning particularly when the majority of these students have to adapt to a completely new system of studying and learning (i.e. critical thinking) in their Higher Education. As this study focuses on British academics who teach in British International Branch Campuses, the contribution by Hofstede plays an important part in investigating how it affects both teaching and coping with student interaction.

It was shown in the preceding literature that academic research undertaken was limited in overseas branch campuses. This study investigates the implications of this and how it affects the British expatriate academic given that research is a necessity for promotion in the UK. How does this affect their chances of returning back to the UK HE sector? It is also highlighted in the above literature that teaching can be challenging in an overseas environment. How does this affect the professional role of the expatriate academic? Research has indicated that there are often increased levels of administration duties that academics have to conduct in an overseas environment. This study investigates how it affects the workload of the expatriate academic. Comparisons in all three core academic roles are made to their previous experiences of working in the UK HE sector.

PART THREE

2.19 The Framework of Five Essential Elements (2007)

The Framework of Essential Elements model was developed by Gappa et al (2007, p.134) to conceptualise and help understand academic professional work. This framework is important to my research study as it relates to the five essential core areas of academic work as well as the linkage to the culture and uniqueness of the University. The framework is based on literature in a Western environment and is relevant to this research as the UAE education system is modelled on a Western education system (Austin et al, 2014). Secondly, as the study aims to compare academic experiences between working in the UK and the UAE, the framework is ideally placed to make comparisons using this model.

The framework was applied in a recent UAE research funded project (Chapman et al, 2014) examining expatriate academics working in UAE federal (public) and state (semi-public) Universities. It is particularly relevant to this literature review as the intent is to focus the study on expatriates working in IBCs. It will also further contribute to research previously conducted by Chapman et al (2014) on expatriate academics.

The literature provides discussion of the framework (provided below) and research where it has been applied to-date.

**Framework of Essential Elements
(Gappa et al, 2007, p.134)**

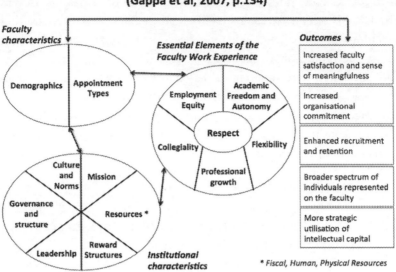

Gappa et al (2007) posit that faculty are the University's most important and major asset – "indeed the faculty's intellectual capital, taken collectively, is the institution's foremost asset" (p.4). Their model incorporates faculty characteristics, institutional characteristics and essential elements of faculty experiences and outcomes that are based on 'respect', which is core to the underpinnings of their model. In the framework, faculty characteristics influence the academic work experience and can alter academic perceptions. For example, the faculty may comprise of varying proportions of either permanent or part-time faculty that can influence both the academic and student experience (Gappa et al, 2007, p.133). Institutional characteristics comprise of culture, mission, governance, leadership and reward – this also varies across schools/departments (Gappa et al, p. 135). Gappa et al (2007) in their research argue that shared governance between administrators and faculty is an essential element to ensuring that the University meets its expected goals and objectives.

The authors' refer to the five essential elements as "benchmarks for examining the strengths and weaknesses of faculty workplaces in institutions and for gauging the extent to which institutions are strategically utilising and supporting the talents and abilities of all faculty members" (Gappa et al, 2007, p.138). Although, the framework is subjective in nature there is an attachment of analytical discipline and simplicity that can be applied to the five core elements and can provide a useful focus for the researcher. In the model, respect is referred to as "the basic human valuing of every faculty member. Respect underlies all institutional efforts to provide an academic work environment that stimulates personal and institutional growth and success" (p. 139). In **employment equity**, the model refers to all faculty members being treated fairly (including part-timers) where faculty have the necessary resources to conduct their job. **Academic freedom** and **autonomy** refers to the right of freedom for academics in their teaching and research. **Flexibility** provides academics with the scope to maximise their work and lead personal lives to the full. **Professional growth** enables academics to gain satisfaction from their work by improving their knowledge, skills and to address concerns. In terms of **collegiality**, this is concerned with developing a community of respect for individual contributions. Gappa et al (2007) recommend that all elements must be in harmony to ensure organisational commitment and achieve institutional excellence – for example, "fair treatment that does not include either collegiality or the opportunity to grow professionally is of little value" (p.142). One fundamental assumption from the model is that the authors recommend that part-timers become involved within the institution and receive the same basic rights as those on permanent positions. The authors stated, "When institutional leaders recognise the value of nurturing a community that includes all faculty members, regardless of their appointments they enhance institutional health and success" (p.20). The framework was applied by the researchers to examine the professional role of overseas academics.

The study conducted by Chapman et al (2014) involved thirty-seven expatriate academics working in the UAE HE sector in public and semi-public Universities. Their study's purpose was to investigate professional employment based in the UAE. The main results indicate that the short-term three-year residency contract (which is linked to UAE Labour Law) promotes uncertainty and "in turn, universities tend to attract instructors who have little interest in a long-term commitment to the institution" (p.141). In this sense, Chapman et al (2014) argue that this is a self-conflicting goal – they question how can institutions expect to become world class research institutions if the expatriate academics are employed on short-term contracts. The authors suggest serious implications for PhD supervision if academics were to leave halfway or cannot inspire long-term commitment that is essential for corporate governance. The study has also raised questions on the lack of staff induction, not involving staff to feel commitment to their institution, and also revealed that research was not important at these Universities or higher education colleges. One of the interviewees refers to research as "it is an afterthought" (p.148). Several constraints such as heavy teaching loads (70% - 80% of their time spent on teaching), lack of research assistants, limited availability of research funding and weak research collaboration were barriers to research progress in the UAE. In addition, academics found difficulty accessing journals and publications (p.144). Those who did research tended to do so to develop or maintain their career mobility if they wished to return back to their home country.

2.19.1 Collegiality

This was mainly across the academics themselves (horizontally - where a positive and friendly atmosphere existed) but not vertically (Chapman et al, 2014). Top-down decision-making was dominant and normally led to senior management informing the academe about decisions and issues. The authors stated, "This top-down model seemed to have a dampening effect on broader collegiality" (p.144). In addition, given the broad range of expatriate nationalities this contributed to constrained collegiality.

2.19.2 Autonomy and academic freedom

The expatriate academics felt comfortable teaching in the classroom but had less autonomy in curriculum development and academic freedom. Some of the interviewees felt that to either criticise or provide academic debate would cost them their jobs and their contracts would not be renewed.

2.19.3 Professional Flexibility

This was a negative given the fact that academics were employed on a short-term contract for three years. "Some went as far as saying that people are fired not based on merit but rather … on politics and loyalty" (p.146). The authors argue that this has an important influence in pushing for changes to working conditions.

2.19.4 Participation in Governance

Short-term contracts made limited sense in involving academics in the governance of their Universities. The findings indicated that academics were more devoted to their students as opposed to the governance of the University.

2.19.5 Professional Development Opportunities

Many interviewees considered this to be superficial and not tailored to their individual needs. When training did take place, consultants from outside the UAE did not fully understand the challenges that expatriates were facing in their training programmes. Consultants lacked the cultural understanding necessary to tailor the training.

The study conducted by Chapman et al (2014) is important for the UAE Higher Education sector and for broader implications relating to other countries involved in transnational teaching. Reliance on expatriate academics (given short-term contracts) cannot lead to developing world-class institutions if there is not a long-term strategy in place to keep and maintain these academics and create organisational commitment necessary to build research. Chapman et al (2014) argue that by creating job security for expatriate academics they can go far in contributing to organisational commitment and in turn enabling the enhancement of institutional quality and research. They also suggest that this study raises similar issues to other developing overseas countries where contract-based academic positions are on the increase.

2.20 Higher Education Sector in the United Arab Emirates

The United Arab Emirates (UAE) currently has a population of 8 million people and comprises UAE nationals (15%) and expatriates

(85%) respectively (UAE National Bureau of Statistics, 2013). The UAE is a Muslim country that observes Sharia Law and is both politically and economically stable. The country has diversified its economy in the past decade from predominately an oil production state to focus on tourism, finance, logistics and the services sectors. Higher Education is one of such services and is expanding rapidly to cater for the population growth and towards a more diversified and knowledge based economy. Transnational higher education contributes therefore as a means to developing a skilled workforce and has been established as a global education hub. According to Lane (2011a), the establishment of private sector HEIs in the UAE serve "public policy goals related to economic development and building capacity within the postsecondary sector" (p.1). Lane's findings suggest that IBCs improve the UAE's "education-related reputation and signalling to the world that it is modernising its economy and its desire to be a regional hub. Thus, IBCs not only increase local capacity and provide a different type of education, but are intended to foster new regional interest in pursuing an education in the host country" (p.1). Thus, the policy has a bearing on the recruitment and retention of high skilled professional labour force. Lane (2011a) posits that "IBCs provide a relatively inexpensive way for governments included in this study to increase capacity" (p.376).

According to the UAE National Bureau of Statistics (2013), there are currently over 100 institutions (70% are foreign branch campuses) catering for 120,000 higher education students. The federal universities (financed and sponsored by the UAE government) account for 40,000 of these students (34%). Emirati students make up 90% of this population. The non-federal universities and higher education colleges are referred to as private higher education providers and are to a large extent financed entirely by student fees and which mainly expatriate students attend (i.e. those non-Emirati students who grew up in the UAE but do not hold UAE citizenship. One of their parents or sponsors must be currently employed or have a business located in the UAE). Thirty-seven international branch campuses (represented from eleven different countries) currently operate within the UAE (OBHE, 2013). Non-Emirati students are taught largely by expatriate academics (QAA, 2014). The international branch campuses are located largely in two free zones (the main free zones being Dubai International Academic City and Knowledge Village), which attract tax exemptions and encourage growth via cluster development by providing infrastructural support and purpose-built facilities (Lane, 2011a).

The Knowledge and Human Development Authority (KHDA, 2013) reported that there are 22,000 students located within the free zones (representing thirty-three institutions). These institutions which operate in free zones are exempt from the federal scrutiny that the UAE government has developed by the Ministry of Higher Education to regulate and oversee the quality of higher education. For example, in the Dubai free zones, Knowledge and Human Development Authority (KHDA) oversees the quality of its providers via the University and Quality Assurance International Board (UQAIB). The UQAIB operates an 'equivalency validation model' which ensures the same quality assurance equivalence that operates in Dubai parallels to that of its home campus. The federal universities (Zayed University, Higher Colleges of Technology and the UAE University) are self-regulated whereas all other non-free-zone universities come under scrutiny by the Ministry of Higher Education under the Commission for Academic Accreditation (CAA) representing 75,000 students. It is proposed that the federal universities will also fall under CAA scrutiny in 2015. The recent QAA Transnational Review in 2014 estimates that there are now over 15,000 students who are studying for a British degree award which is the largest foreign country provider delivering its degree programmes within the UAE. The three largest IBCs based in the UAE are Heriot Watt University Dubai Campus, Middlesex University Dubai Campus and Bolton University Ras Al Khaimah Campus.

The UAE is host to one of the highest percentages of International Branch Campuses (IBCs) in the world (37 out of a total of 200) according to The Observatory on Borderless Higher Education (OBHE, 2014). The term IBC is defined by the OBHE (2014, p.1) as "A higher education institution that is located in another country from the institution which either originated it or operates it, with some physical presence in the host country, and which awards at least one degree in the host country that is accredited in the country of the originating institution". There are several characteristics, which

53

are common to IBCs operating in the UAE. Firstly, UAE institutions operate in the private sector and income is derived largely from student fee income (Clarke, 2013). Secondly, competition is highly competitive and institutions have to operate similar to a business organisation (Clarke, 2013). Thirdly, the facilities (i.e. library and teaching rooms) and academic support infrastructure are below par compared to Western Universities (Clarke, 2013). Fourthly, private sector institutions that operate in the UAE are mainly teaching-led Universities that conduct very limited research output. According to Clarke (2013), this does not inform and enhance teaching and undermines dissertation supervision particularly at Masters degree level. Finally, IBCs comprise largely of expatriate students and international students who are largely recruited by overseas agents.

The growth rate of a number of the IBCs has been particularly spectacular. For example, Heriot-Watt University Dubai Campus was established in 2005 and ten years later hosts over 4,000 undergraduate and postgraduate students in its own dedicated campus (Clarke, 2013). The academic staff that are employed at IBCs are largely expatriate academics who originate from a wide source of countries. The UK, USA, Australia, India, Canada are the main degrees offered by the IBCs in the UAE..

Expatriate students who attend IBCs mostly originate from Indian nationality followed by Pakistani and Arab (non-Emirati) origins. Many of these students were born in the UAE and also attended private sector schooling based on rote learning. International student originate from a wide spectrum of countries with the largest inflow being from African countries. Wilkins and Balakrishman (2011) argue that IBCs based in the UAE need to pay great attention on student satisfaction that result from good quality teachers, good resources and utilisation of information technology. According to the researchers, these factors "could result in significant competitive advantage by improving student retention and student achievement and attracting new students through positive word-of-mouth" (Wilkins and Balakrishman, 2011). Clarke (2013) also confirms this to be highly important in attracting new students. He suggests that staff need to listen carefully to student needs as it plays a vital role in Middle-East culture.

2.21 Main Findings of the QAA (UAE)
Transnational Review

The UAE Overseas Transnational Review conducted in 2014 by the QAA was timely in writing this Chapter. It is important for this research study as it reveals problems concerning academic staffing levels, meeting student needs and maintaining standards (QAA, 2014). Similar issues are identified in the QAA Overseas Transnational Review conducted in China (QAA, 2013). The QAA (2014) found that their experiences with adjunct (part-time) academic staff to be below expectations. Adjunct faculty are often recruited informally and provided with no training support and development. The QAA team also "noted differential approaches to academic self-governance, which is integral to academic culture" (QAA, 2014, p.19). The QAA noted that UK Universities can do more to improve the overall UK academic culture via greater academic involvement. They also noted that the academics based overseas had very limited input into curriculum design and little or no input into moderation or the setting of assessment. Research was also very less transparent compared to the UK HE environment. The QAA recommended for the overseas academe to become much more involved in the UK academic governance (structures, committee and processes) to improve the UK culture for British Universities operating within the UAE. In addition, there was lack of student feedback in place and occasional feedback given to academic staff on external examiners reports. The facilities as well as career and counselling guidance were less comparable to those at British University campuses (QAA, 2014).

2.22 Comparative Summary of the Literature

The following table provides a summative comparison of the literature for the role of the academic working in the UK HE sector and for those British expatriate academics based in transnational higher education. The core role components focus on teaching, research and administration. In addition, this Chapter provided a summary from the literature on the main challenges facing overseas academics, which is available in Appendix Six.

Table 2.1: Similarities/Differences in the Professional Role of UK Academics in Comparison to the Expatriate Academic Community

	Academics working in the UK HE Sector	Expatriate Academics in Transnational HE	Comments
Research	Research output is the normal path for career progression. UK research active staff would not tend to work overseas as it would be a barrier for their career prospects. The UK HE sector up until now does not place significant value on the international experience of an academic who has worked abroad. The UK Research Councils have set clear requirements on the type of research expected which limits and constrains the autonomy of researchers towards pursuing safe research. The UK HE sector is diverse in nature. At one extreme there are universities that are research intensive and to the other extreme there are teaching only universities.	Very limited (or does not exist), particularly in private sector HE providers that tend to focus more on teaching. From the studies reviewed there appears to be a common theme that academics do not have the time to conduct research given the extent of their teaching and administrative duties. If providers do conduct research, it does not occur until the campus is fully developed and has reached full maturity. The literature indicates that research funding is often scarce and that research collaboration is weak. The literature also indicates that British academics that work overseas tend to be those academics that have not been research active.	Clear differences exist in the literature between academics working in the UK and overseas. The lack of research culture in transnational higher education has serious implications for dissertation supervision at Masters level as well as enhancing teaching pedagogy via research-led teaching. Some critical voices suggest that this has serious implications for delivering quality higher education compared to western higher education. Others are critical that lack of research undertaken is a missed opportunity in further advancing the country's development and economy.

Teaching	Many factors have shaped and influenced the teaching pedagogy of academics working in the UK. Whilst teaching hours have actually dropped class sizes have expanded which has impacted the way that academics teach and has added extra workload due to increased assessment marking. In addition, academics have been faced with the challenges of teaching international students and a wider diversity of students. Academics have had to learn new technology in the classroom together with reform of the curriculum to improve graduate employability. There is a growing trend in the use of part-time or fixed term appointments.	Studies have indicated that academics receive limited or no induction in teaching students at overseas campuses. There are numerous studies that highlight the concern that academics are faced with stress and frustration (particularly in the early stages of their appointment) as they need to adjust their teaching pedagogy accordingly and find suitable examples or cases. Research indicates that academics tend to teach in the way that they have been taught themselves which often causes difficulty for overseas students as their society learns differently compared to western societies. In addition, overseas academics have to work hard at building and maintaining relationships with their counterparts in the home campus. Several studies have shown that distance and communication are important for the overseas campus to be successful. Academics often see themselves as inferior to their counterparts as they are normally excluded in developing the curriculum that is standardised. It is common to employ part-time faculty.	In cross-examining the literature available it appears that the role of the academic is challenged in teaching at both home or host campuses. Teaching complexities vary according to the environmental influences. It is hard to assess the degree of difficulty involved given that there are no available studies that have investigated this research question. Across both locations there is a growing concern in the employment and usage of part-time faculty. In not developing the curriculum and with limited or no research it would be an interesting question to assess how this affects the credibility of the academic profession in transnational higher education.

Administration	An audit culture has developed in which academics are scrutinised in their work both internally and externally via government organisations such as the QAA and the student body, which nowadays has a powerful influence over academic performance in the UK HE sector. Managerialism has been introduced into the sector adding new policies and procedures that creates additional administrative duties and workload for academic staff. A major study has shown a slight decrease in the satisfaction level of the academic community over a fifteen-year period.	The literature suggests that academics working overseas often take on greater administrative duties particularly in the development stages of a start-up campus operation due to limited resourcing being made available. In addition, few studies have shown that administrators working in overseas operations are often not as experienced, empowered and competent as their counterparts in the home campus. Often academics are heavily involved in marketing, admissions, timetabling, handling student complaints and overseeing the administration of exam boards.	Both groups are facing increased administration in their work environment. It is difficult to distinguish if one group has a greater workload in this area than the other. It would be interesting to compare experiences to see if one work environment is more challenging than the other.

2.23 Research Gap

According to Kim and Locke (2010), very limited research has been produced to date on the transnational academic profession despite academic staff being the most critical resource that has contributed to the growth of overseas higher education. They posit, "as a result, assumptions about, for example, the international migration of academics, the conditions favouring and inhibiting mobility, the nature of international experiences in their host institutions and countries and the broader impact of academic mobility on styles of scholarship

58

and intellectual traditions, remain largely unexamined" (p.27). In studying the experiences of British expatriate academics working in UAE IBCs this will further the contribution to the knowledge and understanding of academics working overseas and build upon the existing literature. There is an obvious gap in the literature to compare and contrast academic experiences of working in the UAE against their experiences of working in the UK HE sector as identified in the previous section. To date no study has ever been conducted in this field. In addition, more recently Chapman et al (2014) studied expatriate academics working in UAE public and semi-public higher education organisations. Their research applied the Gappa et al (2007) Framework of Essential Elements as a useful means to investigate and explain academic experiences. Conducting similar research of British expatriate academics using the same Framework of Essential Elements as that employed by Chapman et al (2014) will contribute to forming the complete picture of all three types of universities that operate across the UAE HE sector (i.e. public, semi-public and private sector universities).

The next Chapter explains and justifies the research stance and the methods for conducting this study.

Chapter 3

RESEARCH METHODOLOGY

3.1 Introduction

In this Chapter, I explain and justify the chosen research design, methods and research questions. Accordingly, this Chapter is structured as follows. In section 3.2, the study explains the relevance and significance to the field of international transnational higher education. Section 3.3 introduces the research question(s) and links these to the research gaps identified in Chapter Two. My epistemological position is presented in section 3.4. The study uses an interpretivist approach and provides its advantages and disadvantages. In section 3.5, the study explains the research design applying Maxwell's (2005) Interactive Model of Research Design. This study has used a qualitative approach as discussed in section 3.6. Section 3.7 explains the ambiguities and limitations of employing a qualitative approach. The study explains in sections 3.7 and 3.8 respectively methods that were employed. The study used three British overseas branch campuses and covers fourteen in-depth semi-structured interviews. Appendix One indicates the person attributes in terms of HE experience of respondents (both before leaving the UK and of their experience working overseas). Purposeful sampling was employed for this sampling method to select British expatriate academics working in the UAE and who have worked previously in the UK HE sector. Section 3.9 explains the data collection method used in this research study and how the study addressed issues in conducting my interviews. The data analysis is explained in section 3.10 and describes the stages using NVivo. Validity and reflexivity are discussed in section 3.11 to address bias using an interpretative approach. I found the Onwuegbuzie and Leech (2007) 'Qualitative

Legitimation Model' (p.237) useful by adopting seven out of their recommended twenty-four strategies to research methodology and these contributed towards strengthening my validity. Finlay's (2002) map of five variants of reflexivity was also applied to the research design to improve upon reflexivity. I adopted ethical principles developed by Bell and Bryman (2007, p.71) to the research study in section 3.12. Finally, in section 3.13, this discusses the semi-structured interview, which is based on the literature examined in Chapter Two and research questions from section 3.3.

3.2 Justification of the study

The study examines the professional role of British expatriate academics working in overseas branch campuses. This is conducted in the United Arab Emirates (UAE), which is currently host to the largest concentration of IBCs worldwide (Lawton and Katsomitros, 2012). The growth of transnational higher education has simultaneously led to the increase of academics being employed as expatriate staff within IBCs (Altbach, 2002). There are few studies capturing the role of the academic in a transnational higher educational setting (Knight, 2013), which is why the study intends to pursue a research study within the UAE given its dominance and importance. The professional role of the academic for this research is broken down into teaching, research and administration (Barry et al, 2003). One of the main reasons why there is lack of research to date is because transnational higher education is a relatively recent phenomenon – it has only developed and grown rapidly over the past decade.

Maxwell (2005) refers to the goals of research as "to include motives, desires and purposes – anything that leads you to the study or that you want to accomplish by doing it" (p. 15). This serves essentially two key purposes:

a) Is it worthwhile doing?
b) It justifies the research study while simultaneously helps to reduce validity threats encountered while undertaking the research study.

I more recently conducted a small-scale pilot study at an IBC located in the UAE examining the role of the expatriate academic (Clarke, 2012). In the conclusion section of my research, I argue that a larger study in the UAE would help explore this area in greater depth magnifying the research problem further – do all expatriate academics face similar challenges in their role given the international context? How does the role differ to academics working in western Universities?

Working in transnational higher education is an interesting but highly complex environment to work in and differs in many aspects to the home campus (Clarke, 2012). Other key goals of this research are two-fold. In producing this research, I will become more aware of the nature of transnational higher education and this will subsequently contribute to furthering career expectations whilst also developing my research capability. I have worked in the transnational higher education sector for the past decade in senior management roles located in both the Sultanate of Oman and United Arab Emirates respectively. Strauss (1987) suggests that is worthwhile for researchers to make good use of their experiences. "Experiential data should not be ignored because of the usual canons governing research (which regard personal experience and data as likely to bias the research), for these cannons lead to the squashing of valuable experiential data. We say, rather, 'mine your experience, there is potential gold there!" (p.11). It is for this purpose that expatriate academic experiences will be useful in sense making and interpreting the data once collected. As Maxwell (2005) stresses personal motives can have validity consequences in the conclusions of the intended study and I therefore provided reflexivity in all stages of the research design to reduce bias throughout my study. Secondly, transnational higher education continues to grow yet limited research has been conducted to-date on the academic role – hence; this research study will make a contribution to the transnational higher education literature.

3.3 Research Questions and the Research Gap

According to Maxwell (2005), the research question should help focus the research study to a practical size. O'Leary (2004) suggests that it defines the investigation and provides direction. The research question investigates an issue and provides practical insights drawn from the findings. To date, there are few studies exploring the role of expatriate academics, which is why a country specific study is needed given the growth of transnational higher education. It is anticipated that this research will be helpful for home and host campuses in staff planning and for policy makers to alleviate some of the problems identified from this study.

The primary objective of this research study are:

> Using an interpretive approach, the research aims to investigate the professional role of the British expatriate academic working in the UAE – specifically looking at teaching, research and administration practices and comparing and contrasting their UAE experiences to their experiences of working in the UK HE sector. Previous literature and the Gappa et al (2007) Framework of Essential Elements are used as a core element of the conceptual framework as it helps the reader to understand academic professional work.

The primary research question is:

> **How does the overseas conditions and environment affect the professional role of the British expatriate academic?**

The sub research questions are:

1. What are the living experiences of the British academic community prior to and joining the UAE IBC? (In the work/ non-work context).
2. What experiences do the British expatriate academic community face in their pedagogic practice? How does this compare and contrast to working in the UK HE sector?

3. What experiences do academics face in conducting research in the UAE environment? How does this experience compare and contrast to research practice in the UK?

4. What are the experiences of academics relating to administrative duties at UAE IBCs? Are these experiences comparable or contrasting to the UK HE sector?

5. How does the Framework of Essential Elements (collegiality, employment equity, flexibility, academic freedom and autonomy, and professional growth) compare and contrast between the UAE and UK HE sectors?

6. To what extent does the international experience of the academic contribute to their future career aspirations?

The next section discusses the epistemological stance that has been applied in this research study – to understand the professional role of British academic expatriates based in the UAE.

3.4 Epistemological Position

Epistemology is the study of knowledge. It essentially enables the researcher to explain what embraces knowledge and the understanding of the phenomenon. Easton (1998) posits that it is important for all researchers to clearly outline their epistemological standpoint for "claiming to know what we know; the substantive basis of our knowledge claims" (p. 73). Roberts et al (2009) develops this concept further by emphasising that "it is important to understand that the research may also be affected to a significant extent by the philosophical disposition of the candidate. The research beliefs are more likely to affect the area chosen as the basis of research", (3, p. 4). According to Roberts et al (2009), epistemology can either be positivism or phenomenology/interpretivism. Positivism examines the relationships or causality between data sets – for example, interest rate rises and the price of houses can be investigated to see whether there is a correlation between the two sets of data often based on large samples. This is a research philosophy that applies more to sciences or engineering. The researcher is therefore isolated from the sample (in positivism) and is less likely to have an influence on the outcome of the results/findings.

This is where phenomenology/interpretivism is better suited. According to Roberts et al (2009), "most phenomenologists would argue that a purely positive approach does not allow the flexibility and detail required to understand human behaviour" (3, p.10). Phenomenology/interpretivism involves the researcher dealing directly with the sample and focuses on meaning. It develops an holistic approach exploring the totality of the situation and can provide a more detailed understanding into the inter-related causal relationships. As Roberts et al (2009) argue that, "a major aspect of phenomenology is that it is holistic. It addresses a much wider range of different variables than positivism, and it seeks to understand the complex linkages that exist between these variables" (3, p.19).

Some of the weaknesses of the phenomenology/interpretive approach are that it may lack rigor due to the problems associated with sample size and there could be questions as to the interpretation – "the researcher interprets observations and results on the basis of his or her knowledge and experience" (Roberts et al, 2009, 3, p.20). In addition, can different researchers undertaking the same study interpret the same data identically? "Even experienced researchers are sometimes guilty of allowing bias to react with the research", (5, p.34). This can lead to problems of reliability where positivism has an advantage over this approach. However, on the whole, phenomenology/interpretivism can be useful in exploring complex social relationships. Bryman (1984) advocates "qualitative researchers produce data which they often call 'rich' by which is meant data with a great deal of depth" (p.79).

I have selected an interpretive approach as this research study involved the investigation of the understanding of the professional role of British expatriate academics working in the UAE. The researcher has chosen a qualitative approach as described in section 3.7 (Proposed Research Design). Tsang (2013) argues that "interpretive sense making method is more interested in seeking an in-depth understanding of human experience embedded in a rich, real world context than contributing to the development of any abstract theory or concept" (p. 198). The research needs to demonstrate reflexivity when using interpretivism - "this view is borne of the assumption that the prior knowledge, experience, and attitudes of the researcher see things but also what he or she sees" (Bryman and Bell, 2011, p. 30). In addition, Bryman and Bell (2011) argue that interpretivism requires strategies to overcome reliability, replication and validity to ensure warranting and robust conclusions are developed. This will be discussed in detail in section 3.11.

3.5 Proposed Research Design

I utilised Maxwell's (2005) Interactive Model of Research Design in this research design as it is useful for two key reasons:

1) It identifies the key issues of the components of research design.
2) It stresses the flexibility and interactivity of research design decisions.

Maxwell (2005) argues that using sequential models are not appropriate for those researchers using qualitative research. Instead, he advocates that the stages are on-going and interactive referring to the analogy of an elastic band where the stages "can stretch and bend to some extent, but they exert a definite tension on different parts of the design, and beyond a particular point, or under stresses, they will break" (p.6). Maxwell's approach is depicted below in his "Interactive Model of Research Design" (p.5).

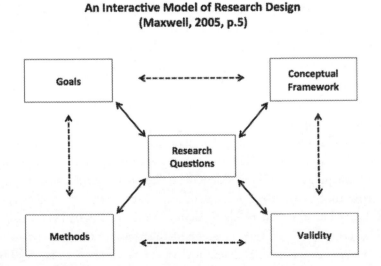

An Interactive Model of Research Design
(Maxwell, 2005, p.5)

In applying Maxwell's model, I assured that there is a high chance of replication of the results (improving validity) by assuring that this study was conducted in three British IBCs. I conducted fourteen semi-structured interviews with British expatriate (UK citizens) academics who were working in UK branch campuses. In thirteen of the fourteen respondent cases they had worked for a minimum of five years or more in UK higher education before working overseas. This was an important criterion to this investigation as several of the interview questions sought to compare the experiences of the respondents to working in the UK HE sector. Appendix One indicates the NVivo person classification and highlights that (apart from one respondent) all respondents had worked in the UK HE sector for greater than 5 years. (Specific details are discussed in sections 3.7, 3.8, 3.9 and 3.10 respectively). In section 3.2, I described my justification and goals of research. Maxwell (2005) refers to the goals of the research as "to include motives, desire, and purposes – anything that leads you to the study or that you want to accomplish by doing it" (p. 15). In section 3.3, I presented my research questions, which as Maxwell (2005) suggests are a key factor in the research design and links to all processes in the Interactive Model. They often can specifically alter the data collection and analysis stages. The Conceptual Framework is essentially looking at the problem and the literature from past researchers. This must be critical and identifies "what problems (including ethical problems) there have been with previous research and theory, what contributions or holes you have found in existing views, and how the study can be made as an original contribution to our understanding" (Maxwell, 2005, p. 35). Gappa et al (2007) "Framework of Essential Elements Model" has been employed as part of my research design. This was discussed in the previous Chapter. In addition, experiential knowledge (what I bring to the study) can lead to possible bias. Critical voices (Denzin and Lincoln, 2000) argue that this actually enhances the research process as my experience, the pilot study conducted previously in assignment three (Clarke, 2013) and familiarity with the literature on transnational higher education have all contributed to my study.

3.6 Qualitative Approach

I chose to follow a qualitative approach as it focuses on meaning, people and situations. "Qualitative research is deemed to be much more fluid and flexible than quantitative research in that it empathises discovering novel and unanticipated findings and the possibility of altering research plans in response to such serendipitous occurrences" (Bryman, 1984, p. 78).

According to Maxwell (2005), qualitative research has eight key benefits:

1. It can provide for deeper meanings and behaviours to those academics being studied in my research.
2. It can help me to understand specific contexts within this study on how academics act. Using a small number of academics to be studied allows me to gain much deeper insight and understanding rather than using large samples where the meanings cannot be deciphered.
3. It can identify unanticipated behaviours not intended in this research study. This is due to the nature of the Interactive Model itself as it is highly flexible and adaptable.
4. It allows me to be involved in the research process as the interviewer.
5. It can reveal causal explanations if the data is coded correctly.
6. Results and findings are made credible to the interviewees and the reader.
7. It can help to improve existing practice as opposed to simply accessing it.
8. It makes this research study credible working within the academic community.

3.7 Ambiguities and Limitations of a Qualitative Approach

Miles (1979) who is one of the leading experts on qualitative research suggests that the method itself has many limitations. He argues that the approach can be very labour intensive and time consuming in conducting the interviewing, writing up, coding and performing the analysis. He also advocates that it can be a stressful activity. One of the main dangers of this method is that there are often few guidelines for the researcher that could lead to "self-delusion, let alone the presentation of "unreliable" or "invalid" conclusions to scientific audiences. How can one be sure that an "earthy", "undesirable", "serendipitous" finding is not, in fact, wrong?" (p. 590). Cassel et al (2006) conducted a study of forty-five qualitative researchers and found that researchers were not applying solid criteria to their assessment of qualitative research compared to quantitative research. They recommended that better-informed training be provided for qualitative researchers. One reflection, I have conducted three qualitative research studies to-date and have received comprehensive training in qualitative research whist attending several workshops. I also attended two NVivo for Mac workshops (Basic and Advanced) prior to commencing analysis of my data set.

3.8 Methods

I planned my research design to focus on the three British IBCs based within the UAE. Within each IBC, I selected British expatriate academics for interview, totalling fourteen interviews. This sample size follows best research practice recommended by Piekkari et al (2009). According to Eisenhardt (1989, cited in Piekkari et al, 2009), this research design approach allows for the researcher to increase the robustness of his findings by the nature of replication. As in Maxwell's (2005) Interactive Model, this helps to improve overall validity and is the reason why I selected this approach. According to Maxwell (2005), "structured approaches can help to ensure the comparability of data across individuals, times, settings, and researchers, and are thus particularly useful in answering variance questions, questions that deal with difference between things" (p. 80). He also stated, "Unstructured approaches in contrast, allow you to focus on the particular phenomena being studied, who may differ from others and require individually tailored methods", (p. 80). I have chosen to utilise a combination of the two techniques above – semi-structured interviews to improve validity but at the same time increasing the opportunity to explore the phenomena with greater depth whist probing further on specific responses (Bryman and Bell, 2011). Bryman and Bell (2011) refer to the semi-structured interview as where "the researcher has a list of questions on fairly specific topics to be covered, often referred to as an interview guide, but the interviewee has a great deal of leeway in how to reply" (p. 467). Bryman and Bell describe the process as being a "semi-flexible" approach to gathering data. A full detailed semi-structured interview for this research study can be found in Appendix Four.

Maxwell (2005) suggests that qualitative methods be established into four sections:

1. Research relationships.
2. The participant selection and/or other sources of data to collect (see Section 3.8).
3. Data Collection (see Section 3.9).
4. Data Analysis (see Section 3.10).

I carefully reflected on intended research relationships and decided not to use my own organisation in this research study. As a Senior Manager of an IBC, I recognised the challenges that would be faced in interviewing colleagues that could lead to possible bias.

3.9 Study Population – Who to Interview?

The study population is British expatriate academics working in Higher Education Institutions throughout the UAE. The criterion was that they must have previous teaching experience in the UK prior to working at the branch campus. I used purposeful sampling to represent expatriate academics from the three British Universities based in the UAE. According to Maxwell (2005), particular persons are "selected deliberately in order to provide information that can't be gathered as well from other sources" (p.88). One of the disadvantages of this sampling method is that personal judgement in selecting interviewees could be wrong. Maxwell (2005) argues that there is no guarantee in that the participant views are representative. According to Maxwell (2005), purposeful sampling serves several purposes:

1) Achieving the 'representativeness' of the population will help provide greater confidence in the conclusions.

2) Selection of interviewees that represent possible variations, which ensures that conclusions incorporate one-offs and provide for greater validity.

3) Access to extreme interview cases can often help to test out theories.

4) It can help to identify comparison, to explain the reasons for differences between individuals in the study.

I attended several academic conferences over the past several months to recruit interviewees for this research study. In addition, I have made several contacts within the UAE academic community over the past six years. British expatriates academics were interviewed, specifically those academics that have held previous positions at UK Universities to enable the interviewee to compare and contrast their experiences in the academic role. Patton (2002) refers to this specifically as 'extreme or 'deviant' case sampling where the strategy is suggested as in some way richer by providing extreme cases (p. 231). For example, two of the respondents had come to the UAE on their spouse's visas and took up employment after settling in. Their experiences were different to that of the other academics settling-in.

3.10 Data Collection

Fourteen face-to-face interviews were set up at mutually convenient times between the interviewer and interviewee and each one lasted for approximately forty-five minutes. Face-to-face interviews were used for this study as they "capture the meaning and interpretation of phenomena in relation to the interviewees' worldview" (Easterby-Smith, 2002, p.144). Prior to the interview, I informed the interviewees about the main purpose of this research study, how their feedback would be used in developing findings and the adherence of strict confidentiality. The interviewees were sent the purpose of this research, the approximate duration of the interview information, what happens with the results of the study and intent to publish results. I also provided a statement to the interviewee that they could withdraw from the research process at any stage in the process. All interviews were recorded with the interviewee's permission and transcribed into a written account using Dragon Dictate speech recognition software. A copy of the transcript was sent to the interviewee to verify the accuracy of the interview record.

3.11 Data Analysis

Notes and memos were also maintained while conducting interviews, transcribing and reading them. Maxwell (2005) empathises that this is an essential requirement to the analysis of qualitative data. He cites "You should regularly write memos while you are doing data analysis: memos not only capture your analytic thinking about your data, but also facilitate such thinking, simulating analytic thoughts" (p. 96). Easterby-Smith (2002) recognises the difficulties in analysing data to achieving both validity and reliability. He stresses the importance of the researcher being always objective and neutral whilst interpreting the research.

I conducted open coding then axial coding, then selective coding to analyse the data set. According to Strauss and Corbin (1990), open coding is "the process of breaking down, examining, comparing, conceptualising and categorising data" (p. 61). My categories were initially analysed and are presented in Appendix Two. These were broken down into the professional role (with sub-categories), the expatriate career and the greatest challenges that the expatriate academics faced.

I then moved to the next step of coding – axial coding. Seale (1999) describes this as a "method of integrating analysis through connecting categories – by deploying as a general frame of reference the context, conditions, strategies and consequences that characterise interaction" (p. 85). For example, I connected both teaching and research categories together (axiom coding) and was able to demonstrate that this had a negative effect on the supervision of Masters Dissertations – without informed research, how could academics conduct their supervision role effectively? Selective coding involves "integrating the analysis even further around a 'core' category – that is, a central concept selected to act as a fulcrum around which others can be brought together into a coherent whole" (Seale, 1999, p. 85). Seale (1999) posits that selective coding provides for niche and more meaningful analysis of the data and can often lead to producing substantive recommendations from this study. For example, selective coding suggests that this will prove a major problem for expatriate academics if they are to return home as research plays a vital part in the careers of UK academics.

I employed the use of quotations in my research findings and analysis because this "will demonstrate reflexivity and awareness of the researcher-subject relationship by showing that he or she has been aware of the power relations between the researcher and the people being studied and has sought to deal with by 'giving voice' to participants in a way that is not medicated by his or her own interpretation" (Bryman and Bell, 2011, p. 702). Finally, I utilised the NVivo (version 10 for Mac) software package in my data analysis, which helped me to be highly productive given the size of the data set (totalling 77,000 words in the transcripts).

3.12 Validity and Reflexivity

Validity, reliability and flexibility are important factors that determine both the robustness and trustworthiness of a research study. Bryman and Bell (2011) describe validity as the "integrity of conclusions that are generated from a piece of research" (p. 42). Essentially, could a study be replicated to produce similar results by another researcher? According to Scheurich (1997), the researcher undoubtedly brings both conscious and unconscious input into the interview, which can affect the interaction involved between the interviewer and interviewee. I gave this careful thought and consideration by carefully playing back recorded interviews to reflect on my respondent interaction and made even greater effort by listening to the interviews to adjust my interview-techniques. For example, I was able to adjust my probing and questioning into areas that produced richer findings based on the research and sub-questions. Reliability on the other hand examines if another researcher could repeat the study results (Bryman and Bell 2011). This methodology has been designed to be replicated by a different researcher in a different country.

Onwuegbuzie and Leech (2007) have developed a useful model called the "Qualitative Legitimation Model" (p. 237) which aims to integrate several of the validity types developed from critical voices on the subject of validity. They argue that there are "threats to the internal and external validity at the three major stages of the process" (p.233) (i.e., research design/data collection, data analysis, and data interpretation).

Internal credibility in qualitative research corresponds to the internal replication of field studies conducted in qualitative approaches (Onwuegbuzie, 2003). Onwuegbuzie and Leech (2007) state, "internal credibility can be defined as the truth value, applicability, consistency, neutrality, dependability, and or credibility of interpretations and conclusions within the underlying setting or group" (p. 234). For example in the case of researcher bias, this could occur at one of three stages (data collection, data analysis and data interpretation) as I (the researcher) was responsible for all three stages. They argue that external credibility "can be generalised across different populations of persons, settings, contexts and times" (p. 235). Onwuegbuzie and Leech (2007) identified 24 strategies from critical voices in the qualitative research field. I carefully selected six that applied to this research study:

1. Member checking (explained earlier).
2. Making comparisons – using the three British IBCs helped me to enrich the data set just as that used in quantitative research. In addition, the findings were compared to the existing literature.
3. Checking for representativeness – this was improved by involving a larger sample in qualitative methods (fourteen interview participants).
4. Checking the meaning of outliers – I paid attention to exceptions (thus helping me minimise any illusory correlations).
5. Replicating a finding – the larger the population, the more confident I was about the findings and legitimation.
6. Peer debriefing – colleagues and supervisors were asked to examine data, analysis and findings to verify the validity of study and the recommendations that are developed from findings.

A definition of reflexivity is "the ability of the researcher to stand outside the research process and critically reflect on the process" (O'Leary, 2004, p. 11). Reflecting on oneself as a researcher allows us to critically understand how knowledge comes into existence.

I have over ten years of HE work experience at three International Branch Campuses (based in the UAE and Sultanate of Oman) and ten years of HE experience working in the UK. This has directly shaped my perspective and knowledge of the comparison between the home and host campus. I was familiar with all substantive findings and research studies on academic challenges and issues having conducted early pilot studies in the UAE.

Finlay (2002) developed a map of five variants of reflexivity which offers the researcher both opportunities and challenges. He posits, "Assuming it is even possible to pin down something of our inter-subjective understandings, these are invariably difficult to unfold, while conferring to methodological inadequacies can be uncomfortable" (p. 212).

3.12.1 Reflexivity as an inter-subjective reflection

The aim was to extend beyond self-reflective consciousness whilst I recognised that my familiarity of the subject area was a possible bias threat. Johnson and Turner (2003) suggest that it can be an advantage for the researcher as it can lead to deeper and enhanced research and "will raise it to consciousness and use it as part of the inquiry process" (Reason, 1994, cited in Maxwell, 2005, p. 38). My familiarity greatly assisted me whilst conducting the interviews, as I was able to probe further in the questioning. It also greatly assisted me to analyse and interpret the data set.

3.12.2 Reflexivity as a mutual collaboration

This is a useful approach that involves the participants in the study to become involved in the interpretations of findings/results and recommendations. According to Finlay (2002), it can provide for a more complete application of the process of reflexivity itself. I employed this technique in my research plan. Two of the fourteen interview respondents provided valuable insights on the interpretation of the findings and helped to articulate some useful and practical recommendations. Johnson and Duberley (2003) describe the process in psychological terms, "A researcher engaging in epistemic reflectivity adopts a participatory approach to increase awareness of their own habitus processes. It requires cooperation." (p. 1293).

3.12.3 Reflexivity as a social critique

How did I intend to manage the power relationship between myself (the interviewer) and the interviewee? I treated the interviewee as 'equals' for the purpose of this research study. My own organisation was not therefore part of my research inquiry as it would involve the manager-subordinate interaction. This greatly assisted me in reducing any concerns that my relationship would have in the interview process.

3.12.4 Reflexivity as discourse deconstruction

How questions are asked can impact on interviewee perception. This is why there is a need to play back the interview recordings and carefully review and reflect. According to Finlay (2002, p. 225) reflexivity can produce the following benefits in research:

- "Examine the impact of the position, perspective and presence of the researcher.
- Promote rich insights through examining personal responses and interpersonal dynamics.
- Open up unconscious motivations and implicit biases in the researcher's approach.
- Empower others by opening up a more radical consciousness.
- Evaluate the research process, method and outcomes.
- Enable public scrutiny of the integrity of the research through offering a methodological log of research decisions".

3.12.5 Reflexivity as an introspective perspective

My experience allowed me for greater insights into the study itself and was helpful in the interpretation of the meaning from the data and the linkage between claims, warrants and knowledge. Participant and supervisor involvement in the interpretation of my findings and recommendations reduced potential bias.

3.13 Ethical Issues

Sin (2005) argues that research ethics should not be treated as a separate section in the research process but rather throughout the entire research process itself. For example, ethical issues may arise in gaining access to potential interviewees, in the interview itself, reporting the findings and the power-relationship of the interviewer/interviewee.

I followed the ten categories of Ethical Principles adapted by Bell and Bryman (2007, p. 71) in my research study:

1. I did not harm any participant (both physically or psychologically).
2. I respected the dignity of the participants involved in this study.
3. I respected participant privacy.
4. I upheld confidentiality (for both the individuals and IBC – no names will be mentioned nor names of IBCs).
5. I conformed to anonymity.
6. I never lied or deceived the interviewee.
7. I did not hold any conflicts of interest in my research study.
8. I ensured trust, honesty and transparency in all stages of my research process.
9. I provided reciprocity to the benefit of both researcher and respondent in transcript and available findings.
10. I avoided misrepresentation and avoided false reporting of the findings.

3.14 Semi-structured Interview Questionnaire

The semi-structured interview questionnaire is based upon a combination of the literature review, the Gappa et al (2007) framework examined in Chapter Two and research questions discussed in section 3.3 of this Chapter. The interview questions were divided into ten themes, which proved a useful start to helping me analyse the data set within the NVivo software package. I will now discuss the formulation of questions; a full copy of semi-structured interview questionnaire is presented in Appendix Four.

3.14.1 Theme 1 – Motives for working overseas

This set of interview questions determined the specific reasons for moving abroad and proved useful in assessing and comparing the findings to the original research conducted by Richardson (2000). The interviewees were questioned on their previous UK employment, their experience of working in the UAE and other overseas countries as this helped me to understand, analyse and explain the underlying motives for working overseas. The duration of overseas experience was important in helping me to connect linkages to the other themes from this study.

Question One – What were your primary motives for working overseas?

Question Two – Were you previously working in an HE sector in which you were research active or based upon a teaching only employment?

Question Three – How long have you been working in the UAE? Any previous overseas HE experience?

3.14.2 Theme 2 – Moving abroad and settling in

This theme investigates the experiences that expatriate academics face before moving to the UAE, the level of support provided by their University and how they have coped and adjusted to their new environment. It addresses the literature on pre-departure training (Richardson and McKenna 2002; Schermerhorn 1999; Chapman and Austin 2002; Bodycott and Walker 2000; Dunn and Wallace 2006; Woodhouse and Stella 2008) and culture shock (Lane 2011a; Schermerhorn 1999; Bodycott and Walker 2000; Gopal 2011). The theme is important to this research study as it helps to explain the nature and challenges often faced by expatriate academics in moving abroad and to draw comparisons to the literature in the analysis.

Question Four – What personal challenges did you (and your immediate family) face in moving abroad and settling in? Did you face any form of culture shock? Does it still exist?

Question Five – Did you receive any pre-departure training or training when you first joined the campus?

3.14.3 Theme 3 – Comparing teaching overseas to the UK

Teaching is a core component of the professional role of an academic. This theme captures the two sides of teaching in the UK in contrast to teaching overseas. The literature suggests that teaching overseas is very challenging (Macdonald 2006; Richardson and McKenna 2002; Pyvis 2008; Dobos 2011; Lane 2011b; Teekens 2003; Crose 2011; Devitta 2000; Woodhouse and Stella 2008; Crossman and Burdett 2012; Dunn and Wallace 2006; Gabb 2006). No specific studies to date have compared this yet there are many studies available which suggest numerous challenges such as difficulties in teaching pedagogy, and the implications of using a standardised curriculum and assessment strategy.

Question Six – What have you found to be the key differences in comparing your teaching experience overseas to your experience of teaching in the UK?

Question Seven – How do you feel about delivering a standardised curriculum and assessment strategy? To what extent does the curriculum and assessment tailor to the needs of your students?

Question Eight – Have you faced any stress in your classes? If so, what were the causes?

Question Nine – How have you coped with student interaction? (Both inside and outside the class).

3.14.4 Theme 4 – Comparing research overseas to the UK

The research studies (Macdonald 2006; Barry et al 2003; Richardson and Zikic 2007; Welch 1998; Fielden and Gillard 2011) and table 2.1 of comparison of the research undertaken in Chapter 2 clearly indicates the lack of research culture that exists in transnational higher education. The following questions seek to confirm this but also probe further into its implications and how expatriate academics feel about how this affects them and their future career aspirations.

Question Ten –   How does research differ here to the UK? What are the barriers and constraints to undertaking research?

Question Eleven – What implications does research have for you and to your institution? How does it affect your future career aspirations?

3.14.5 Theme 5 – Comparing administrative duties to the UK

In Chapter Two I compared and contrasted administrative duties and suggested that one could not fully assess whether the duties were more challenging compared to the other. The following questions sought to discover this and at the same time provide further insight to an area in which very limited research has been conducted to date in transnational higher education.

Question Twelve – How do your administrative duties compare to the UK?

3.14.6 Theme 6 – Relationships with the home campus

In Chapter Two I examined the literature on the relationships between the host and home campuses. Several studies (Hughes 2011; Eldridge and Cranston 2009; Smith 2009; McBurnie 2000; Harding and Lammey 2011; Pyvis 2011) indicated that poor relationships can affect the operations and can be stressful for both administrators and academics. Distance and poor communication links were also important aspects leading to the deterioration of the relationship and a cause for the perception of poor quality. Several studies cited about the 'parent versus child' relationship. The next questions probes this theme further as it helps me to explore the environment and conditions in which the academic is facing.

Question Thirteen – How would you describe your relationship with your colleagues at the home campus? How do time, distance and communication mediums play a role in this relationship? What tactics have been used in addressing them?

3.14.7 Theme 7 – Comparability of the academic professional role applying the Framework of Essential Elements

In Chapter Two, I selected the Gappa et al (2007) Framework of Essential Elements model as it helps one to understand and compare the professional role of the academic operating in both UK and UAE HE sectors. The next set of questions is specific to this Framework.

Question Fourteen – How would you describe collegiality in your workplace and how does it compare to your experience of working in the UK HE sector?

Question Fifteen – How would you describe academic freedom and autonomy in your workplace and how does it compare to your experience of working in the UK HE sector?

Question Sixteen – How would you describe professional growth in your workplace and how does it compare to your experience of working in the UK HE sector?

Question Seventeen – How would you describe flexibility in your work place and how does this compare to your experience of working in the UK HE sector?

Question Eighteen – How does employment equity here compare to your experience of working in the UK HE sector?

3.14.8 Theme 8 – Resourcing and its impact on the role of the expatriate academic

It has been suggested in the literature that resources (e.g. counselling, career guidance, facilities etc.) are not equivalent to those at the home campus. From personal experience and observations I am aware that academics will often have to guide students on non-academic related matters when more often these services are limited or non-existent. In addition, heavy reliance on the use of part-time faculty lowers the overall student learning experience and more often permanent members of academic staff have to pick up student queries outside the classroom when part-time faculty are not present on campus. The next questions examine how this affects the professional role of the academic.

Question Nineteen –   How does resourcing affect your role in this campus?

Question Twenty –   What are the implications of using part-timers for your role? Is this comparable to the UK experience?

3.14.9 Theme 9 – Career expectations and future plans to move back to the UK or another overseas country

Richardson and Zikic (2007) in their research implied that expatriate academics could face difficulties in returning to UK higher education, as they would have to leave their current job to return home without a job. Given that the research culture is limited in transnational higher education does this make it even harder to return back into the UK higher education sector?

Question Twenty-One –   Having moved overseas how do you think your career expectations compare to those if you had remained in the UK?

Question Twenty-Two –   Would you think it easy or difficult in returning back to the UK HE sector?

3.14.10 Theme 10 – Greatest challenge affecting expatriate academics

The final question is important as it helps to prioritise from the sample their greatest challenge working overseas and compares it to their greatest challenge whilst working in the UK HE sector.

Question Twenty-Three –   What is your greatest of all challenges facing you in your role? What was your greatest challenge that you faced in your previous role whilst in the UK HE sector?

3.15 Concluding Remarks

In this Chapter, I focused on the methodology and research design for my research study. I thoroughly enjoyed conducting the interviews. All respondents were very open to recording these. I felt that my utilisation of applying semi-structured interviews helped to provide me with a structure to the interview itself but also provided me with considerable flexibility. The transcribing was very labourious and took up a large part of my time. Using the NVivo package helped me considerably to analyse the 77,000 dataset much more quickly than I had set aside for. It is an easy package to master and greatly aids one's productivity in the research process. I regret having not used this to prepare my literature review chapter. If I were to have done this research again, I would have added a few focus groups as it would have strengthened the research design.

The next Chapter discusses the findings and analysis of the fourteen interviews conducted.

Chapter 4

THE ACADEMIC ROLE UNDER THE MICROSCOPE – FINDINGS AND RESULTS

In this Chapter, the researcher discusses the findings and results of his fieldwork data that was structured around the themes developed in Chapter Three. Interviewee quotations are used throughout this Chapter to illustrate and capture the experiences of those academics interviewed in this study. Section 4.1 identifies the key motives for moving and working overseas. This highlights that the primary motives for working overseas have slightly changed over the past fifteen years when comparing them to the study undertook by Richardson (2000). The background profile of the academics that had previously worked in the UK highlight that they had come mainly from a teaching-focused University followed by those academics who have worked previously in a FE/HE college. It is unlikely for academics that have come from a research-intensive University to work in transnational Higher Education. Section 4.2 explores the experiences of academics moving abroad. It demonstrates that a number of challenges are faced in first arriving at the campus and settling in, causing anxiety and stress. The evidence reveals that there is a lack of support provided by all the branch campuses in this study to help new academics settle-in smoothly into their transition. In addition, very limited induction and mentoring support are in place to help prepare the academic for their new role and support them to adjust to their new environment.

Section 4.3 explores how teaching in the UAE differs to their UK experience. The maturity levels of students can be challenging in adapting a suitable teaching pedagogy. The students come mainly from a background where rote learning (memorisation) is embedded in their schooling background making it challenging to teach a British curriculum which embeds and practices critical thinking and independent learning. The British academics working overseas struggle to move students to a state of critical thinking and independent learning and this can be challenging for new and existing academics in the classroom. The findings in this section highlight three variations in which the curriculum and assessment strategy is devised and implemented across the three British branch campuses in this study. The standardised system adapted by one branch campus creates a sense of deskilling of teaching in the classroom and leads to difficulties in implementation. Academics favoured their autonomy when the uniform curriculum and assessment strategy did not apply in one of the branch campuses. Section 4.4 examines the key differences in research practice between the UK and their overseas experience – research is rather limited in the UAE branch campuses and can affect the future career aspirations of expatriate academics. Administration is explored in section 4.5 suggesting that this function of the academic role is more demanding in the transnational higher education setting. Investing in the support and infrastructural services of overseas campuses can support academics to help them focus more effectively on teaching and learning. One of the overseas campuses that was studied in this research invested more resources into this and this has reaped rewards for both staff and students alike. Section 4.6 addresses an important framework (Gappa et al, 2007), which is used to analyse the academic role. The relationship with the home campus is examined in section 4.7; for some academics they have faced negative experiences. Section 4.8 reviews career expectations of expatriate academics and assesses the perception if it is easier or more difficult to return back to the UK HE sector. In section 4.9, the researcher examines the key challenges faced by academics. Section 4.10 provides a summary of the key findings.

4.1 Motives for Working Overseas

The dominant reason for working overseas in this study was to seek out a new adventure. Over half of all interviewees cited this as their primary reason for moving abroad:

> **Interviewee 2:**
> I have been working in the UK for sometime. In my previous job, I worked for five years. I kept on renting other people's houses. When I saw the job advertised, the adventurous person in me decided to apply.
>
> (Appleby University)

Three interviewees who fall into the category of 'adventure seeking' were also motivated to move out of the FE/HE sector to work in a University environment and saw this as an opportunity towards gaining career advancement. One further interviewee was working in the FE/HE sector but came to the UAE via her husband's sponsorship.

> **Interviewee 9:**
> I was in the same job for about 15 years and could have been there in ten or twenty years' time. My father was here working in the 1970s. That's when I saw a few adverts in the Times Higher and Times Educational Supplement. I was single, tax-free I suppose. I was looking for a change, an adventure really.
>
> (Beta University)

> **Interviewee 7:**
> Good question. Think back twenty years … why did I go to Hong Kong? Curiosity? Chance of a promotion moving from a FE/HE college to University teaching.
>
> (Beta University)

Both Interviewer 7 and 9 reflect a growing trend in which academics who were previously working in the FE/HE sector are moving into transnational higher education. Five further categories were identified from the fieldwork data. Firstly, two of the interviewees stated that they had been brought up in an overseas environment during their childhood and this was their primary motive to move abroad:

Interviewee 10:

Well, I think, because I have lived abroad when I was a kid, and I enjoyed particularly when we lived in a hot country and I enjoyed the heat. So it was literally everything to live abroad rather than the work; it was finding a job that would mean I could live abroad in another county, preferably a hot country. So, that was it really – just more lifestyle.

(Appleby University)

Interviewee 6:

My parents lived here for the best part of 20 years. So, I spent a lot of time here. I have always been looking for the right type of academic role to come back here to work. So, that's the first thing but also, if I am being honest … when I was in the UK, competition for research was too high. I felt that.

(Appleby University)

Interviewees 6 and 10 felt the need to move back to their original residence as they both found that it could provide them with a better lifestyle than in the UK. Two interviewees stated to the question that they had moved to the UAE initially through their spouses and then took up employment at a local University when they arrived:

Interviewee 3:

Okay, well the original reason we came here was in fact connected to my wife's work actually. So, if you like, it was an indirect decision where the opportunity came up for her as a HR director with her company for MENA. Yeah, I think, it was a good time to go because for me I got this job initially part-time at the University and we brought our daughter with us.

(Beta University)

One of the interviewees stated that his motive for moving abroad was to raise the family in a Muslim society and to enable him to pursue research where he could not do so at his previous University based in the UK:

> **Interviewee 5:**
> Personal was about starting a new life with my wife. Part of the reason coming to Dubai is that it is halfway between the UK and Myanmar so it is midway for both of us to start a new life. I think the career related ones … I have handled programme management previously in the UK. I wanted a change before I get back to conduct further research. I did not have the chance to publish since completing my PhD and I saw the opportunity in coming here to achieve this.
>
> (Appleby University)

One of the interviewees stated that his primary motives for working overseas was to find a full-time position whether it was locally or abroad:

> **Interviewee 8:**
> My primary motive was to get a job because I have worked back in the UK teaching part-time … in the downturn of 2008. It got more difficult and I sought looking for a full-time teaching position. I could not get a full-time job at a University and I therefore started applying further and further afield. I didn't really think about it until I got an interview and then I thought about it more seriously.
>
> (Appleby University)

In the case of Interviewee 8, pressures to find a full-time job were upmost which resulted in the need to work overseas. The final category for motives came from one interviewee who was approached by the home campus and asked if he would like to work abroad in their UAE branch campus:

> **Interviewee 11:**
> So it was not really anything planned … I mean one of my colleagues approached me in the corridor and asked me, "we have just opened a new campus in the UAE. Would you like to consider it?" Also, because my religious background is Islam and I always wanted to see how things are in the Middle East.
>
> (Charleston University)

In the case of Interviewee 11, the prospect of working in a Muslim society was important to him and the upbringing of his family. The findings of the fieldwork agree with the Richardson (2000) study of thirty expatriate academics that the primary motive for working abroad falls into the 'adventure seeking' category. However, what is different than Richardson's study is that new categories have formed fifteen years later. We have seen the emergence of academics wanting to work overseas where they originally grew up and the trend that FE/HE academics are recognising overseas HE employment as a way to enable them to move into University teaching. In addition, there is the opportunity to find employment in the HE sector (either part-time or full-time) if the spouse finds work in the UAE in the first instance. As more branches increase, it is likely that academics will be approached by their home campus to work overseas. A breakdown of where the interviewees originally worked in the UK highlights an interesting finding revealing the type of academic who works overseas.

Of the fourteen interviewees studied, one came from a research-intensive University, ten came from a predominantly teaching-focused University and the remaining four came from where they were teaching HE programmes in an FE/HE College. For the one interviewee who had worked in the research-intensive University he was eligible for the previous RAE in 2008 but had not reached professorial status at that stage. This is similar to the Salt and Wood (2014) findings where few research active academics tended not to work abroad.

4.2 Moving Abroad and Settling In

There is a clear contrast between the experiences of those who moved abroad with their spouses to take up employment later in the UAE and those academics that were employed directly by the University. The two academics that arrived with their spouses came via either a multi-national organisation or local organisation, which provided support on moving, housing and settling their children into school:

> **Interviewee 12:**
> There were no problems moving here for us. It helped having a good Public Relations Officer in the organisation and he helped all of the guys and wives as well. He sorted schools, driving licenses, bank accounts … We were very lucky really as I have known others to find it a real struggle.
>
> (Charleston University)

> **Interviewee 3:**
> I would say it all ran very smoothly indeed … The others well, horror stories or difficulties.
>
> (Beta University)

In both interviews above, respondents recognised the problems that their colleagues had faced in moving abroad if they were employed directly by the University. For those academics who were employed directly by the University, conditions such as setting up a bank account, having a medical examination, organising the visa, finding schooling for children all proved significant challenges resulting in some of interviewees developing stress and anxiety. These academics had to simultaneously start a new job, a new way of life and make new friends:

> **Interviewee 10:**
> I think it is just sort of starting off from scratch, you know, on a completely blank slate. You have to build it up from nothing. So, the biggest thing that I really felt was the social side of having no connections and it did take a good two years to get a social circle.
>
> (Appleby University)

For this interviewee, it was a personal challenge in terms of being exposed to an environment where there was no social circle in place when she first arrived. She experienced loneliness at the beginning in contrast to her previous social life in the UK where she has a circle of closely established friends.

> **Interviewee 1:**
> One was the heat and the other was the speed at which things get done here. It is really a big hurdle to get things started such as setting up a bank account to getting your diplomas attested. The rules constantly change which is frustrating. Also, accommodation was provided for me in my first overseas employment here but it was not what I expected compared to back home.
>
> (Appleby University)

Interviewee 1 was frustrated and anxious in her tone at how long it took things to get done. She compared her experience to those in the UK, where services were performed much more quickly. Obtaining an employment visa can take up to one month. This involves finger printing, undergoing a medical examination and the submission of documentation such as attested degrees. Without this in place, expatriates cannot open a bank account or obtain accommodation or place their children into schools. This has been a reoccurring problem faced by academics and has led to stress and anxiety and also affecting their family (if they joined them):

> **Interviewee 4:**
> The visa is the one thing that can greatly be improved because you cannot get an UAE driving license unless you have a visa in place. So that means that you cannot hire a car and it even means that you cannot register your children to any schools. This has been greatly worrying for my family.
>
> (Appleby University)

Interviewee 4 argued that this was one of the greatest personal challenges that he and his family faced. These settling-in challenges, which the British academics face in the UAE, are not dissimilar to that which has been described in the literature previously (Richardson and McKenna, 2002). They still exist today despite recommendations suggested by the above researchers. Coupled with lack of proper induction programmes and formal mentoring systems (that exist in the majority of experiences described by the interviewees), it further adds to the anxiety and stress placed upon the expatriate academic. The findings from the fieldwork data clearly indicate that similar patterns have not changed since over a decade later when Chapman and Austin (2002) argued for better training and support to be given to overseas academics on joining their University:

> **Interviewee 1:**
> There has been no formal induction or mentoring in place for the three Universities that I have worked for in the UAE.
>
> (Appleby University)

> **Interviewee 6:**
> There was absolutely no training or mentoring provided … I think it is unprofessional to go that far.
>
> (Appleby University)

In the above interview, the interviewee described his negative experience of not being picked up at the airport despite being told he would be by his University. It was noted that the interviewee was negative towards his present University as he was expecting a more positive experience and support to be provided in the early stages.

> **Interviewee 14:**
> We did receive some basic documentation about life in the UAE before joining … you know about the facilities that are available and the kind of things you have to do. A limited bit on cultural aspects but not too much. I think they kind of did not want to scare people away so it is why they don't give you much until they come.
>
> (Beta University)

This reconfirms what other interviewees have stated earlier. The major finding is that no training is in place or it is conducted superficially. Despite the lack of limited induction available, there were positive signs shown to welcome a family provided by the account of one interviewee's experience for his first overseas posting:

> **Interviewee 7:**
>
> I guess the induction programme for wives, which was good. That was the kind of an informal thing where other wives have established over the years – it worked as a network.
>
> (Beta University)

This highlights from interviewee 7 that personal attention makes a difference in welcoming family members and can have a positive impact in how the family settles in. Beta University had more recently set up a one-week induction programme. When asked if it had included training related to pedagogical teaching areas or cultural training, it was more based around administrative and IT library and e-learning systems training:

> **Interviewee 14:**
>
> We did get a one week's induction ... My impression is that they kind of expect people to stand on their feet. Maybe, they recruit taking that into account as well. They tend to recruit people living here locally who are already used to living here and understand how it all works.
>
> (Beta University)

This highlights that Beta University has learned that it is better to recruit expatriate academics that have had previous transnational higher education experience, as they will be able to adjust to their environment much more quickly. Several of the interviewees did face stress in the initial stages of joining their University in teaching:

> **Interviewee 2:**
>
> The first few weeks of teaching there was an issue. The conduct of the students and facing Asian students for the first time did not go well.
>
> (Appleby University)

For this interviewee, this led to stress and she was thinking of returning to the UK in the first two months of her teaching post. She had been teaching for over thirty years in Higher Education. Others faced difficulties:

> **Interviewee 1:**
> I faced stress particularly at the beginning of my teaching as I found the students to be immature and disruptive in class.
>
> (Appleby University)

> **Interviewee 10:**
> When I first arrived and had to teach on the foundation programme (to fill my hours) … I found this very stressful. Those were the young kids with attitude and I did find that very difficult.
>
> (Appleby University)

The evidence above clearly indicates the need to provide training and coaching/mentoring support for newly arriving academics in handling classes where the students tend to be more immature compared to teaching UK University students. In addition, teaching pedagogy instruction and support is also needed during induction to help the transitional adjustment become smoother. Several of the interviewees stated that they were given modules to teach which were not in their specialism. This also led to stress. The next section will explore how teaching in the UAE Branch Campuses compares and contrasts to teaching in the UK.

4.3 Comparing Teaching Experiences

This section addresses the core function of the academic role – teaching. The field data indicates that there are several areas in which teaching differs. Students studying at the UAE branch campuses largely came from a different schooling system in which memorisation formed the basis of their learning development in contrast to independent learning and critical thinking which are the grounding of the UK schooling system. In addition, many of the interviewees stated earlier that the maturity level of students caused them challenges in the classroom. For expatriate teachers, they often experience difficulties and stress in class:

> **Interviewee 2:**
> The differences are mainly in the types of students concerned. The type of students you get here are not independent learners. They come from a schooling system that depended greatly on their teacher where they memorised or did not reflect upon what they were doing. Yet in the UK, the students tend to learn independently. So here, I find the students more demanding and challenging in terms of their expectations. In the UK, you get the results but with less effort. Here, it is very much a lot of handholding.
>
> (Appleby University)

Interviewee 2 has had over thirty years of teaching experience in Higher Education. The contrast that she makes to the UK HE environment suggests that students need greater support and attention compared to UK students. Interviewee 2 had experienced the impact over this period of massification and diversity of UK students entering into the UK HE sector.

> **Interviewee 12:**
> There is a slight mismatch I would say in the candidates and the tutors need to work a lot harder. Our students (based in the UAE) do not always come from an academic background whereas those students in the UK have come through the A-level route and are therefore familiar and more comfortable with academic writing. So, although we try to maintain a lecture style here, many students require more of workshops and tutorials to underpin what they are learning in class … There is a lot of vocational stuff going on to make sure that the students are up to speed which compares to HND teaching in the UK … We have to do a lot of behavioural or classroom management to manage large classes of disruptive students which can be very challenging for our staff … The behaviour comes from a combination of immaturity and an element of invincibility. They answer their phones in class, would continue full conversations whilst the teacher is still lecturing; they would open their laptops and stream movies during the lecture, so it is quite challenging for staff … They don't want to be here, they don't want to be studying; they want to be out in their 4x4s dune bashing and it is inconvenient for them to be here so they would continue their social lives through the classroom. So, we have to de-programme them when they

> get here. It makes it rewarding in a way because when they go from year one to year three and onto Masters if they want, you see a transformation in the students.
>
> (Charleston University)

Interviewee 12 had described her teaching experience as being similar to that of working in an UK FE/HE college environment. Immaturity levels of students can often cause challenges and stress upon teaching staff. When it comes to results, British based students tended to outperform better to their UAE based students. This was reflected in the majority of views expressed:

> **Interviewee 1:**
> The students in the UK are stronger in terms of critical thinking and more generally get better results. I think at the beginning it is very difficult to understand that students do not read before they come to class; they do not have opinions in class and you often have to repeat the materials in so many ways. At the beginning when results are not good, you start to wonder is it my teaching? After a while, you get to realise that for other academics they are facing the same issues and challenges.
>
> (Appleby University)

For this interviewee, it took almost one year to realise that she was experiencing similar problems faced by her colleagues. One important finding in which several of the interviewees stated was teaching modules that were not in their teaching specialism. This provided a challenge experienced by many of the interviewees and was stressful:

> **Interviewee 1:**
> Here you are a jack-of-all-trades. In the UK, you will teach in a specific subject area but in Dubai, we are considered as generalists and have to teach courses where we do not have the specific subject knowledge and understanding. It is not right for students and not right for academics to be faced with this situation.
>
> (Appleby University)

Interviewee 2:

However, one thing that I really thought, hmm, this is new to me, is in the UK, most of the modules that you teach are your area of expertise. Sometimes, in this part of the world, it might be mix and match, is where some modules is what you wanted and others could actually be something you have to pick up and that was a little bit of a challenge.

(Appleby University)

Interviewee 10:

I did not (with my main teaching subject) which is psychology but when I first arrived, I was also teaching on the foundation programme at Beta University to fill in some time. And that was stressful.

(Appleby University)

All three interviews clearly highlight the differences experienced between the UK HE sector and transnational higher education. For the academics, they are placed in difficult and challenging situations, which are stressful. For the overseas student, they are not receiving quality teaching.

The three British Universities based in the UAE where the research was conducted applied varying policies for the implementation of their curriculum and assessment strategies. Charleston University originally applied a standardised curriculum and assessment strategy which was designed by the home campus. In the past two years, they have allowed the branch to adopt their own materials and develop their own assessments and exam papers under moderation by the home campus (provided that learning outcomes are met). Appleby University has adopted a uniform curriculum and assessment strategy with some contextualisation. Beta University in principal has established a uniform curriculum and assessment strategy but it is not strictly enforced allowing some schools to be flexible in how they deliver their curriculum (i.e. changing materials) whilst having the same assessments and exam papers. In the case of Charleston University, the interviewees have welcomed this change to adapting their own materials and setting the assessment themselves against the learning outcomes:

Interviewee 11:

I mean the freedom that we had in the UK where you just pick up the module specification with the learning outcomes and then it was up to you how to meet that. That little bit of freedom was actually removed here and you have a module box with the slides, the assignments, everything where initially I find it very restricting. Now they have changed that and we have the freedom to develop our own material, which I like.

(Charleston University)

Interviewee 12:

So, it makes the teaching easier for them to engage with. The teachers prefer this. We have access to each other's slides so the UK can access ours and we can access theirs. Previously (in the previous policy) we struggled with the assignments, as it was very difficult for staff and students to understand the impact of a particular industry and the surrounding economy when they were not living in it.

(Charleston University)

Interviewee 13:

There is more freedom to individualise the delivery that has made it easier for students to engage and learn. I have also found it to be less stressful as it takes the home campus away for me to focus on the students.

(Charleston University)

In all three interviews, this move by Charleston University had served both staff and students well. This is an area in which the UK academics have autonomy over; for those academics working at Charleston University they clearly were happy to move to what they originally had experienced in the UK. In contrast to this, Appleby University interviewees have formed negative impressions of having to apply a common curriculum and assessment strategy. Some even have suggested that they have become second-class citizens (similar to the argument put forward by Schapper and Mayson, 2004) due to the deskilling of the academic role in teaching:

Interviewee 4:

I think this applies to most of the institutions and that is the problem because you are teaching as a deliverer of a course rather than teaching as an enhancement of a course basically and there is a big difference. That causes a problem and demotivation. If there are motivational issues, then of course you will deliver to the best of your abilities but you could do better … Personally for me, I think if it is done correctly, it can work but the problem is if the relationship becomes where one campus is basically providing all the material and the other campus is just delivering that, then you have missed out a lot because the person delivering it does not have the ownership of this material, is not part of that process. He may want to change things, he may want to modify things and especially do things when it comes to the assessment. So, if it is an all-inclusive process where the curriculum development, the assessment is done collectively across campuses. It will provide a better curriculum than what is currently produced by people who are in one campus. So, I think it is involvement … Sometimes, I feel like being a second-class citizen.

(Appleby University)

Interviewee 4 felt that he was losing his autonomy and that the process prevented him for playing a part in quality and curriculum enhancement. He felt rather angry, comparing himself as a 'second-class citizen'.

Interviewee 1:

When you are here, you are given a standard set of teaching materials that is not your own material. So, sometimes I think it takes longer to make the materials fit rather than your own material. When you are back in the home campus, you are the one making the decisions on the curriculum. Here, you are teaching something which you might not entirely agree with. I know we have the same quality levels. But when it comes to the same quality levels, the experience is not the same. We have a wide range of students attending branches and learning partners all over the globe. I would like to see a more internationalised curriculum, which will be appealing for people from all over the globe.

(Appleby University)

> **Interviewee 2:**
> Personally, it prevents us from tapping into the international context of the country. The home campus can learn something from us. If you have a standardised curriculum, it is blocking the teacher's mind. I feel deskilling of teaching using standardised slides. It does not enrich my experience. You are following other academic's interests. Modules that could be interesting, you think why am I doing this?
>
> (Appleby University)

In the case of interviewee 2, she felt undervalued as an academic in contrast to her experience of teaching in the UK HE sector.

> **Interviewee 10:**
> Well, it is very difficult; I mean that is the absolute bone of contention and at best least understood by the home campus and the least sympathetic by the UK faculty. The impression is, "oh, but we have sent you everything therefore you do not have any work". And the reality is I have to teach what your brain thinks. I am going to take a week to figure that out so it is very difficult.
>
> (Appleby University)

The above interviewee was very negative on using a standardised curriculum. She was resentful of the fact that her colleague at the home campus perceived that academics at branch campuses had little work to do given that the materials were produced for them. It clearly caused her effort in trying to understand and prepare the slides that the UK academics developed.

> **Interviewee 5:**
> The other thing is my experience so far of aligning of the curriculum. What you get is a set of textbook slides that has got very little room for contextualisation, very little detail. The idea is fine but it is down to the implementation, which is difficult to manage on our side. I feel devalued as an academic.
>
> (Appleby University)

Interviewee 5 clearly was not impressed by the quality and depth of materials provided. He too felt negative towards the effect of deskilling. At Beta University, there were mixed messages as the policy reflected what the school adopted in terms of variability and flexibility in the curriculum:

Interviewee 14:

So here we actually give far more attention than the home campus … Since I have been here, we have made changes to the curriculum every single year. We constantly try to improve the programme. In the UK, they have done nothing. So, that tells you all you need to know … I like my autonomy, I think I have the ability to develop my own materials. I will always respect the assessments and the outcomes. I will make sure that I definitely cover what I need to cover and I will make sure that the students are all prepared for whatever assessments that come their way. Generally speaking, with my colleagues here on campus, I think we share a lot of those beliefs and that helps. We try to customise the curriculum to make it more relevant and also more doable. Some topics which are okay there, they are not okay here either because of cultural or impracticalities.

(Beta University)

In this interview, there were hidden messages revealing that the quality of materials sent by the home campus were not of a standard that this interviewee wanted to provide students. He refers to other colleagues sharing his 'beliefs' that they had to radically adapt them in teaching students.

Interviewee 9:

Standardise from the UK? That has been tricky as well … Follow it – which was initially quite appealing because everything has been prepared but as you go into it after a few years, I would not have done that in the first place but I have to do it anyway … And all of a sudden, we are given the opportunity to set the curriculum and assessment for the MBA programme. It is just like what we always have done back home but you get out of practice after a while.

(Beta University)

The home campus has allowed this branch campus to develop their materials and set assessments for its MBA programme. It is noticeable that in this interview, the interviewee felt out of practice in developing his materials as he was used to teaching a standardised curriculum.

> **Interviewee 7:**
> I think it was a little bit of a culture shock at first. So okay, you are going to teach exactly what we are doing in the UK. Having said that, certainly we found we don't. We teach pretty much what they teach in the UK but we can manoeuvre and whatever else ... as you get to know your counterparts so you have some opportunities to discuss and manoeuvre the assessments.
>
> (Beta University)

The findings from this section clearly reflect the difficulty in applying a uniform curriculum. In cases where this was not applied, academics welcomed their autonomy and felt that it was in the best interests of their students. A grey area exists at Beta University. On one hand, there is evidence that the quality of materials provided by the home campus has made academics adjust the materials to improve upon them. In one exception, autonomy has been fully given to the MBA course team by the home campus. The next section will examine how research compares and contrasts to the experiences of the interviewees.

4.4 Research

The field data clearly indicate that research has taken a minor role at all three British Universities as they focus mainly on teaching, which is clearly more important in a private sector higher education environment. For some of the academics that participated in this study, this posed a major challenge to their future career aspirations and for some there were negative feelings that the lack of research output restricted their chances of returning to the UK HE sector:

Interviewee 1:

In the first University that I worked in the UAE, it was totally a teaching institution where no research took place. In the University that I currently am working in, they are working towards research but in general research is on a backburner. In the UK, promotion is linked to the REF. Here, the position of branch campuses for the REF has been unclear. In the last REF, academic staff could not be submitted from branch campuses. However, most academics felt if they want to return to the UK, they have to have articles to return to a good position. By doing limited research here, you minimise your chances of returning to the UK. Some colleagues have referred to it as being in a loop because as you are teaching more you have less time to spend on research. I have to get my articles. If I don't, I will return to a lower level in academia, which is kind of sad.

(Appleby University)

In this case, the interviewee recognised that her posting overseas had affected her chances of returning back to a good UK University if she does not produce articles. She expresses a tone of negativity towards the situation she is faced in.

Interviewee 2:

Research here is not as well supported as it is in the UK. In the UK, we have a research culture where there is regular research seminars attended by both students and academics alike. Here, it is a bit of an isolated activity. I feel I have lost out in the four years I have been here. I have not been able to do any PhD supervision as I feel I have lost out as I should now be a full Professor. There is a lack of research grants available here in the UAE compared to the UK. In terms of career aspirations, for me I am a fighter, but it is making my fight longer to become a Professor.

(Appleby University)

This interview revealed that there is a clear difference in research undertaken in the UK compared to where she currently works. The respondent originally came from a teaching institution. The interviewee felt that her aspiration to reach professor status had clearly taken a set back with her current position and she could have advanced much more quickly had she remained in the UK (an opinion). This raises an interesting point in how the lack of research culture can influence career progression.

Interviewee 4:

For anyone to come and work within the UAE, this is one of the least preferred places to come at this moment in time. We are the same as a third world country and the main reason for this is that there is no research council which means none of the universities can go and compete for a research grant, publish and do whatever gets done ... In the UK, you have a clear direction of how much research, funding, publications you should have done and that becomes the backbone of your progression to associate or full professor level. It is a clear thing. How many years you take to get there is up to you. Here, there is no research. Somebody joining a University here and I'm not just talking about Appleby University, on what basis are you going to move this guy up to professor level – there is nothing. No research funding means that there has got to be another way to promote these people otherwise they will be stuck in their jobs for the rest of their lives and I don't know what the answer to that is.

(Appleby University)

Those employed at Appleby University are directly employed by the home campus and hold identical employment contracts. This interviewee is despondent as the prospects for career advancement clearly rest on the basis of research output. Given the lack of research at the branch campus, he feels resentment in that the career promotion ladder is not equivalent to his colleagues at the home campus who have much better opportunities to conduct research. Teaching has taken priority at his branch campus.

Interviewee 13:

Oh, it's a huge difference. The expectations for research were very little here because it was a place to teach and teach well. So in fact, whilst I had the research interest, I had to subjugate my time; I had to concentrate more on teaching.

(Charleston University)

Charleston is very much a teaching-led University that places importance on teaching quality. Very limited time is available for research.

Interviewee 11:

Well, I think obviously there is less research opportunity here especially as you are overloaded with twenty hours of teaching. It is always much harder to actually get involved with research and time as well as the resource that is really very limited. So, I feel my research flow has a little bit suffered.

(Charleston University)

This interviewee came originally from a research University in the UK. He felt negative that his career was suffering and has since left Charleston University to take up employment at an UAE University, which has more research activity and time available to conduct it whereas he struggled to cope with too high a teaching load. Research is practically non-existent at Charleston University. At Beta University, research was being introduced gradually but on a smaller scale as teaching again has taken priority:

Interviewee 7:

It's only in the past three years or so, that they (the home campus) have started to become much more research active ... I think we are probably following the same loop here but we are a couple of years behind but more focused now towards research. I'm not saying that there is pressure at the moment here; it has increased this year and last year.

(Beta University)

It is noticeable that teaching loads at Beta University are between 12-15 hours dependent on programme leadership. This interviewee did produce at least one paper per year for a local conference.

> **Interviewee 9:**
> We have done a lot to raise the gravitas if you like for research. Although we are predominantly a teaching institution … it's up to the individuals. There are very small funding grants available if you want to pursue.
>
> (Beta University)

In this case, the interviewee suggested that there is no emphasis placed on research output at present. There were small funding grants available but these required a lot of effort to obtain due to an extensive application process and supplementary documentation.

> **Interviewee 14:**
> I have never done research in the UK. One thing that I would say is that you are limited to an extent here. For example, if you want to do critical research here, you are limited because there can be serious consequences for that … I know somebody not that well who actually lost his job because he was a critical theorist and he just wanted to do some research. He just started asking and looking for a response and somebody took exception to what he was asking and within a week, he had to leave the country. I think he had been here for over twenty years. So, you have got to be very careful.
>
> (Beta University)

This interviewee revealed the nature and extent whereby freedom in research can often be restricted. The Chapman et al (2014) study of the public and semi-public Universities reveals that due to heavy teaching loads, there is limited time available to pursue research. Again, this is very comparable to the findings of this study in the private HE sector. The next section will investigate how administration in the academic role compares or contrasts to the experiences of the British academic.

4.5 Administration

This section provides the findings of the third area of the academic role – administration. There is evidence to suggest from the field data that administration is perceived as more demanding and time-consuming compared to their previous UK experiences as they recalled.

This will be largely dependent upon the nature of the infrastructure invested at the branch campuses in academic support functions such as administrative services, academic enhancement support, careers and other services handling student disability. There is considerably less infrastructure and support at branch campuses in comparison to the UK but it was noted that Beta University did invest more resources into their academic enhancement unit that did help in supporting academics to focus more on teaching and learning (UAE QAA transnational review, 2014). Contrasting this with other Universities, academics had to spend further effort and time themselves in supporting students on referencing and academic writing skills. All respondents from this study stated that there was less administrative support staff based at the branch campuses in comparison to the UK. This often placed greater burden on the academics to provide more administration duties than their UK counterparts. In some cases, academics were expected to attend Open Days and Recruitment fairs on fifteen days per year normally at weekends. Many academics even had to become involved in counselling and provide career support due to the lack of resources available at the branch campuses (in contrast to the UK home based Universities):

Interviewee 10:

The main difference is that in the UK, there was an admin department, which was run by fully qualified professional administrators and have adequate staffing levels. There was an admissions department run by fully qualified personnel. So, they took the decisions and worked independently. Here, our admissions department are not qualified to make decisions and are few on the ground. The academics have to do this for example which increases their workload.

(Appleby University)

In this case, the interviewee compared and contrasted that there was a clear difference in resourcing levels and the quality levels of UK staff being better trained compared to the administrative staff at the branch campus.

Interviewee 5:

We have to provide additional support to students because students come to you and ask how to do referencing more often than the UK. We are quite poor in terms of induction in writing support. In my previous University, we had what we called Helpster and that Helpster is a kind of one-stop shop for all student enquiries to do with academic support … I think it makes my academic role even more difficult. You inevitably find yourself having to fill in the gaps dealing with lots of student queries and perhaps if we had a better infrastructure, it could be dealt with more efficiently and effectively for students.

(Appleby University)

This interviewee clearly was comparing his experience to his previous UK University in which academic support is provided. This lack of support provided by branch campuses adds to the workload of academic staff.

Interviewee 12:

As far as counselling and the other student support services go, we are very lucky to have the NHS, a lot of charities and support by Universities in the UK. They are few and far between here and lacking in qualified counsellors.

(Charleston University)

This quote outlines a clear comparison in the differences in counselling support between the two countries.

Interviewee 11:

In the UK, if you are doing programme management you get hours off your teaching load and things like that. Here, there is definitely an imbalance and no hours are given … In the UK, if students have special needs it is very obvious who to refer them to and you get professional support. Over here, it is really very limited.

(Charleston University)

In this branch campus, academics are expected to teach twenty hours per week and do not get a reduction of teaching hours for programme leadership.

Interviewee 9:

Particularly at Beta University, we do not have a departmental secretary or support staff. It is much more centralised. We have a good academic support unit that helps our jobs enormously in providing support to students. This is important, as I know colleagues in other Universities who struggle without this support.

(Beta University)

In the case above, it highlights the comparison in the support levels at branch campuses compared to UK Universities. The comments made by the above interviewees clearly reflect some of the challenges faced by academics working overseas. They are completely similar to the survey findings made by the Fielden and Gillard (2011) study revealing concerns over the amount of administrative duties performed by overseas expatriate academics given the lack of resources in place at the branch campuses. This field data also investigated the utilisation of part-time academics and how they contributed to additional workload for the expatriate academic. The interviewees have suggested that there is a greater percentage of part-time staff used in teaching modules at branch campuses compared to the UK:

Interviewee 11:

I am the Programme Manager for a programme where half those teaching are part-timers. Students might need time to see them on a one-to-one basis and so I spend a lot of time in trying to support the students myself. Likewise, other full-time academics do this too.

(Charleston University)

This respondent claimed that additional workload was placed upon the full-timers given the heavy weightage placed on recruiting part-timer adjunct faculty.

> **Interviewee 5:**
> There is greater use of part-time staff compared to the UK. Here, sometimes you have issues with part-time staff in terms of standards of teaching, in terms of marking ability. It has affected my role, as I have had recently to re-mark the scripts of a part-timer who has not done their job properly.
>
> (Appleby University)

In this particular interview, the interviewee was particularly concerned with the quality of part-timer marking causing him to mark again 300 exam scripts.

> **Interviewee 1:**
> There are more part-timers here than in the UK. One of the problems facing full-time academics is that students will come to see you if the part-time faculty are not on campus. Students always want answers immediately which create additional workload for full-time members. In addition, you are responsible for all the marks presented to the Board and this creates additional work for full-time academics to check the marks and ensure consistency. Many of the part-time staff may have worked in a different University (American/British/Indian/Australian/Canadian) and it takes time to ensure that marking is consistent. For example, a distinction in the American system is a 90+. Here it is 70+ etc.
>
> (Appleby University)

This academic felt that there was a problem in that part-time faculty did not teach at one University but several. The different University systems operating in the UAE presents challenges for academics in marking consistently and this increases the chances of marking error. Pressure is placed on full-time academics to ensure that academic standards are in place and increased workload is placed on full-time faculty to review their standard of marking and if these have been entered in correctly.

The next section examines how the Five Essential Elements of Faculty Work (Gappa et al, 2007) compares to the UK academic experiences.

4.6 The Five Essential Elements of Faculty Work

The Five Essential Elements Framework developed by Gappa et al (2007) (professional growth, collegiality, academic freedom and autonomy, flexibility and employment equity) is based around respect for all faculties. This section explores this conceptual framework in the study.

4.6.1 Professional Growth

There were key differences between the experiences of those working in the UAE compared to experiences of working in the UK. The UK HE sector provides greater resources for developing staff compared to the UAE academic. The main reason is that the majority of UAE institutions are in the private sector, which means that resources are restricted and limited. In addition, very limited PhD supervision exists in overseas campuses compared to the UK HE sector. However, it has been noted that some staff obtained positions such as Programme Leadership at a much early stage in their academic career that has provided some growth to their personal and professional development. Where training did occur, it tended to be standardised for everyone in contrast to a more tailored approach, which is practised in the UK HE sector:

Interviewee 2:

Our professional growth is not the same compared to the UK when you attend conferences and academic enhancement. You have proper induction, health and safety. So many seminars. Professional growth here is not well planned and developed. The professional growth of academics working here has been much slower compared to the UK.

(Appleby University)

This interviewee enjoyed the development undertaken in the UK and has recognised a clear contrast and underdevelopment in her current posting.

> **Interviewee 1:**
> I think I have grown tremendously here particularly because I left the UK and having just completed my Doctorate. You tend to get responsibility very quickly overseas. For example, course directorship, director of learning and teaching etc. I would not have received this responsibility early in my career having stayed in the UK. However, there is lack of PhD supervision which I kind of regret. There are few formalised training programmes or meeting expenses for conferences that I did receive in the UK.
>
> (Appleby University)

This interviewee obtained a programme leadership role early in her career, which can be a positive feature of working overseas. However, this was counterbalanced by the lack of training, conferences and limited PhD supervision that could help her in her future career advancement.

> **Interviewee 11:**
> Very limited over here. Whereas in the UK, you get to go on conferences and training etc.
>
> (Charleston University)

> **Interviewee 12:**
> Very few externally arranged staff development opportunities here ... Edexcel offer training quite a lot ... we would invite all staff regardless of whether they teach at undergraduate or masters level.
>
> (Charleston University)

It is noticeable that in this case, the University used Edexcel to train all academic staff highlighting the scarcity of resource provided by the branch campus.

> **Interviewee 3:**
> I have not done much of it here. There is too much bureaucracy and form filling etc.
>
> (Beta University)

The interviewee responded in suggesting that the University did not want academics to apply and that funding was limited.

Interviewee 13:

We did have a few in-house training seminars here but it was to make sure that you delivered and taught better. In the UK, it was more tailored to your development needs in addition to staff training.

(Charleston University)

Charleston University focused largely on teaching and learning quality for training and development purposes. Similar experiences were found in the Chapman et al (2014) study, which investigated public and semi-public Universities. Chapman and Austin (2002) have argued for greater investment to develop academics that are involved in working overseas and provide more PhD supervision for research supervisory experience.

4.6.2 Collegiality

Comradeship and professional relationships appear to be similar in the United Arab Emirates to the respondents' experiences in the UK HE sector. However, the opportunity to engage in the development of University planning and policy was missing at branch campuses according to the majority of respondents. Some interviewees commented that closer links existed in the UK between academics and administrators. Vertical integration tended to be one-way whereas there were some channels available in the UK to become involved in departmental planning and resourcing. In addition, it was often difficult at branch campuses to build close-knit teams as part-time faculty tended to only be on campus for teaching classes:

Interviewee 7:

I think it has got a good team spirit and very good interaction between people. I think collegiality is pretty much the same.

(Beta University)

> **Interviewee 14:**
> I feel people have a lot of respect for each other and we get on well. Also, vertically, I feel collegiality is also very good because the management respects people and the power distance is not great.
>
> (Beta University)

It was noticeable that this academic preferred working in this environment where respect for each other was in place.

> **Interviewee 13:**
> I think horizontally, there weren't many differences. But I think vertically, it is slightly different here as you have more direct communication with your line manager whereas it was more bureaucratic in the UK.
>
> (Charleston University)

For this respondent (and others) highlighted that academics are able to easily converse with line managers, as the organisation structures tend to be less bureaucratic, smaller and flatter in structure.

> **Interviewee 1:**
> There is good collegiality existing here and previously where I worked in the UK. The team back in the UK was a close-knit team similar to here.
>
> (Appleby University)

> **Interviewee 2:**
> There may be some cultural differences that affect collegiality. In the UK, there was greater transparency. For example, there was transparency in the timetable and it was more open for academics to discuss. You will be involved somehow in the process.
>
> (Appleby University)

This interviewee stated that decision-making power of academics is practised more in the UK HE sector in contrast to the branch campuses.

> **Interviewee 5:**
> The administrators were quite close to us in the UK and so you build a bit of a relationship socially as well as in meetings. Here, I feel I do not contribute to strategy or direction. There is a lot of communication that comes down and from the home campus but communication does not seem to go the other way.
>
> (Appleby University)

The interviewee had experienced more involvement in his UK University and felt the loss of power that he was previously used to. Similar findings were found in the Chapman et al (2014) UAE study of public and semi-public Universities although respect for academics by senior management tends to be stronger in International Branch Campuses when the literature and these findings are compared.

4.6.3 Academic Freedom and Autonomy

The transcripts indicate that academics have to be careful of what they said in class due to cultural sensitivity within the UAE. The main reduction in autonomy came by delivering the same curriculum for several of the interviewees to the extent that deskilling of their role had taken place:

> **Interviewee 13:**
> I have to be careful when I engage my audience. So if I have a class with Emiratis for example, there are some things that I wouldn't say because that would upset them.
>
> (Charleston University)

In this case, the interviewee revealed that he could not use examples such as alcohol, couples living together or references to gay or lesbian relationships in class. He suggested that he had to be constantly thinking of this in class due to his awareness of cultural sensitivities.

> **Interviewee 1:**
> You are less autonomous here compared to the UK because the curriculum is set by the UK. You can localise a bit but you don't have that freedom. When it comes to setting the assessment the autonomy is also lost. In terms of academic freedom, you have to be aligned to customs, regulations and cultural sensitivity. I notice that my words are spoken carefully. Clips that I would show of 'Little Britain' could not be shown here. I would offend people with it. In terms of research, there are things that I should not research given the cultural sensitivity.
>
> (Appleby University)

For this academic, there were some restrictions in which humour was eliminated from her classes. It made 'awareness' of sensitivity always on the academic's minds during the teaching and learning process. In the above case, this was typical of those employed at Appleby University and highlighted the resentment in the restriction and freedom to teach what one researched.

> **Interviewee 10:**
> Well, as we said earlier, you are not free at all because you are constrained in your teaching. Well, this is the biggest gripe really.
>
> (Appleby University)

The findings are reflective of Dobos's (2011) and Hughes' (2011) research studies in that the home campus often does not listen to the voices of their academics working overseas and often can lead to the deterioration of morale and the sense of feeling unequal compared to academics at the home campus.

4.6.4 Employment Equity

The key difference in employment equity is that of promotions. The lack of opportunity to research at overseas branch campuses places expatriate academics at a disadvantage. Research is a key area for career progression in the UK. Other differences were for part-time academics that were often projected as peripheral to the institutions. They often did not receive any training. In addition, they did not receive housing allowances or severance pay (paid as one month for each year worked in the case of full-time academics). Payment is normally made on an hourly basis. In the private sector, University salary for full-time academics was different and this was compensated with a tax-free salary, accommodation allowance and holidays:

Interviewee 1:

If I compare myself to colleagues in the UK, teaching wise, we teach much more. Administration wise, I think we do some things differently due to lack of resourcing and lack of empowerment in the admin team. However, I think course leaders in the UK will undertake additional responsibilities. They have to do quite a bit of work for all campuses abroad. I think this is not an easy thing to forget. In terms of promotions, we are clearly disadvantaged. In most Universities in the UK, course development can also excel your promotion chances under HERA whereas we are not allowed to be involved in the process. In terms of being part of the University, I feel that we are an afterthought rather than having any say.

(Appleby University)

In the above case, this interviewee clearly indicated her frustration at being on unequal grounds when it came to promotions. Not being able to be involved in curriculum development combined with lack of research opportunities clearly affected one's chances for promotion.

Interviewee 14:

My sister works in education for many years and they have actually good money coming in and will receive fairly good pensions. So, when you don't get the pension you have to sort yourself out.

(Beta University)

This could be offset against the tax-free salary and accommodation allowance provided to UAE expatriate academics.

Interviewee 2:

In the UK, there is a form of clarity. As regards to part-time staff, in the UK, they will be assigned office hours. In our campus, part-time staff have no office hours and they normally work at several institutions. This also has a major impact on the full-time faculty when students seek answers to questions and it steals your time. It also causes anxiety for students as they are being tossed from one pillar to another.

(Appleby University)

Interviewee 2 drew attention to inequity for part-time staff in contrast to full-time academics. She also indicated that there was a problem in that part-timers are not assigned office hours causing extra workload onto full-timers.

4.6.5 Comparing Flexibility

The findings indicate that flexibility is similar compared to the experience of working in UK HE sector. Staff can work from home and in one case was allowed to take a three months leave break in the summer:

Interviewee 2:

Academic flexibility is about the same when you can work from home.

(Appleby University)

Interviewee 12:

A huge amount of flexibility. I've got my hours that I work but as an example, I have the entire summer off. It is unpaid but I get to come back to my job here after the summer. I fly back to England.

(Charleston University)

In this case, she expressed her view that the UK would not allow this to happen.

> **Interviewee 14:**
> Yeah. It is very flexible from a XY theory kind of thing. The assumption is that we are motivated to work and nobody is monitoring us and so forth.
>
> (Beta University)

These findings were similar in all interviewees highlighting that flexibility was very much comparable to their previous UK experiences. It is interesting that the three year visa renewal was not seen as a negative influence for academics working in international branch campuses whereas the study conducted by Chapman et al (2014) raised this as an important influence on short-term continuity of work for those working in the public or semi-public Universities. The next section examines the findings of the relationships with their home campus colleagues.

4.7 Relationships with the home campus

All interviewees made efforts to work with their counterparts to build relationships and felt that this was very important in developing and enhancing effective communications between colleagues. Several of the interviewees who had visited the home campus or academics who had visited the branch campus said that this was a catalyst in developing one-to-one interaction much more quickly. There were some interviewees who did perceive negative experiences of interactions with staff at the home campus as the counterparts were either too busy or not interested:

> **Interviewee 11:**
> For me, it is easy because I have worked over there at the home campus and it makes a huge difference knowing your counterparts. There could be issues for someone who is totally new working here, or never worked in the UK trying to have a relationship. Language barriers and communications barriers may not be helpful.
>
> (Charleston University)

This interviewee recognised that his colleagues could face difficulties in communicating with their counterparts although in his particular case he knew people whilst working beforehand at the home campus before moving to the UAE.

Interviewee 7:

Generally, with the ones I directly interact with is pretty good. Not to say that is always the case. You have to build relationships and once they get to know you and you get to know them, it starts to gel a bit … I don't think 3-4 hours are a big deal but I think the Fridays are a big deal. The trouble is they are working on Friday and we are not and we work on Sunday and they are not. So kinda two days out of the equation. In one case, I got emails from one of my colleagues on a Friday morning, which there was nothing I could do about it. He wasn't gonna do anything until he returned on Monday morning. So, it was last minute because it was an exam question. Normally, if I email people or whatever, I get a next-day response and likewise.

(Beta University)

Whilst communications are generally smooth, there are sometimes occasions when Friday, Saturday and Sunday can be problematic, as there are assumptions to have no communication between the two campuses on these days.

Interviewee 5:

To be honest, okay. Where I have probably had the best working relationship with a colleague whom I have been dealing with on a postgraduate module. We have built up a good relationship, that's fine. I have had incidences where there was some conflict. I think there was one incident where information was overwritten (on VLE) and a very negative email from that colleague came back cc'd to many people. You were almost seen as being kind of a lower level to the home campus.

(Appleby University)

In this case, the interviewee had an example where he faced hostility due to a mistake he made in deleting course material on the Virtual Learning Environment. He felt that he had received a negative experience as their counterpart copied several of her home campus colleagues into the email sent to this interviewee.

> **Interviewee 1:**
> It depends on the personal relationship that you have. It takes time to build that … One thing that I have noticed is that once they have been to the campus their attitude changes. I had one person visit and he has become very helpful.
>
> (Appleby University)

These interviews brought to light the importance in meeting face to face in developing effective communications. The findings are largely similar compared to those made by Heffernan and Poole (2004) and by the recommendations made by Panteli and Tucker (2009). One of the interviewees identified the danger of part-time faculty members having limited time on campus meaning that building relationships with their counterparts at the home campus could be at a potential risk. For part-timers using the phone would also be limited for communication purposes. The next section explores career expectations and future plans to move back to the UK or another overseas country.

4.8 Career Expectations and Future Plans

Thirteen of the fourteen interviewees felt that it would be difficult to return back to the UK HE sector. The lack of research being conducted overseas was the major reason accounting for this. A few of the interviewees did suggest that there may be some possibility to return back to a niche organisation where there were more international students attending at the UK campus. One of the interviewees felt that he would be better placed to move back to the UK HE sector as he had recently taken up his first overseas employment at a British University. When asked about their career aspirations and had they remained working in the UK, several of the interviewees suggested that they would be further on in terms of their career progression. Those interviewees who came from the UK FE/HE College felt that had they remained in this sector they would never go onto to their doctoral studies. In this aspect, they had moved their careers forward by working overseas:

> **Interviewee 2:**
> If I had stayed in the UK, by now I would have been a Professor. I have missed all of the things such as PhD completions, examinerships and journal papers. I'm staying on for a while due to personal circumstances. You need to have 3* or 4* papers to go back. It would be extremely difficult for Teaching Fellows to go back to a good University in the UK.
>
> (Appleby University)

For this interviewee, had she remained in the UK, she felt she would be further on in her career signifying that the move internationally can hinder one's promotion prospects.

> **Interviewee 9:**
> At my age, coming 51, probably really impossible. I would find it incredibly difficult to get back in.
>
> (Beta University)

In this case, the interviewee came initially from a UK FE/HE institution. Given the low profile of his research background this greatly affects his chances of returning back into the UK HE sector.

> **Interviewee 10:**
> I think now returning back to the UK is impossible but I knew that. I never really wanted to go back living in the UK and realistically trying to go back to a UK academic life would be impossible.
>
> (Appleby University)

This interviewee has accepted the fact that their international appointment is for the longer-term and that it was now impossible to return back to the UK HE sector.

> **Interviewee 5:**
> Yeah, very difficult. I think because for a number of reasons. Firstly, publications, those need to grow. Maybe in a couple of years' time, if I have got 3* publications, maybe then that would be easier but the other thing is the UK perception as if you are working in an inferior environment contrast to the UK.
>
> (Appleby University)

It is important to note that this interviewee suggests that there is a perception in the UK transnational HE is inferior. This perception can be negative in returning into the UK HE sector.

> **Interviewee 1:**
> I probably would go back to a lesser position simply because I have not the research articles. It would probably be a step back when I go back. On the social side, you have to adjust to the environment and the way of living.
>
> (Appleby University)

For this interviewee, it was again recognised that research was fundamental to returning back to the UK HE sector. She also felt that she might find it difficult to fit back into the environment comparing her experience when she moved to the UAE.

> **Interviewee 11:**
> I think I have been here for 5 years, I can see myself growing here rather than considering going back … It could be challenging to go into an UK university but my worry is more for my children where I want them to live in a comfortable environment rather than me about my work.
>
> (Charleston University)

In this case, his family has a major influence in remaining overseas, as his children and family have settled in to the environment.

The next section examines the key challenges that the interviewees have faced whilst working both at home in the UK HE sector and abroad in transnational higher education.

4.9 Key Challenges

Appendix Five presents the findings of the key challenges in a tabular format. It depicts the top challenges faced while working in the UK and the top challenges whilst working in a transnational HE setting. All interviewees were asked to compare both challenges and provide which challenge had the greatest impact for the academic. In analysing the data, the researcher has categorised them into several broad categories which is presented in Table 4.1 below:

Table 4.1 – Analysis of Challenges

Challenge	UK Challenge	Overseas Challenge	Greatest Challenge	
			UK	Overseas
Neoliberal forces * Research intensification * Funding constraints * Massification * Teaching International Students * Reduction in Autonomy	8		4	
Work-life Balance	3	3	1	2
Beginning of Teaching (stress)	2			
Moving from University to University	1			
Research – lack of		3		2
Settling-in		3		3
Difficulty in teaching		4		1
Working in a UAE Public University		1		1
TOTAL	14	14	5	9

4.9.1 UK – Greatest Challenge

The interviewees suggested that the impact of neo-liberalisation forces were perceived as the greatest challenge facing the academic working in the UK. Eight out of the fourteen interviewees said that they faced some form of neo-liberal force (research intensification, massification, funding constraints, and difficulty in teaching international students or reduction in academic autonomy) impact, which was challenging and affected their role:

> **Interviewee 13:**
> I think it was the way higher education was going in the UK. Why did I became an academic is because I like freedom. I like the idea of being able to teach what I want to teach. Things became prescriptive. We have to have lesson plans, you have got to do this for this week etc. Autonomy and freedom was being undermined. So, it was more like becoming a business.
>
> (Charleston University)

It does appear that there is a strong influence shaping this interviewee's decision to move abroad. However, this interviewee moved to a private sector University abroad, which at that time had a standardised curriculum in place and operated in an open market structure.

> **Interviewee 4:**
> I think still the 'R' word but you knew there was some light at the end of the tunnel. One of the biggest contributors of research for us would be the EPSRC. Now the funds are getting very tight. So, it is getting harder and harder to get funds. So, we had to go to the European Union or maybe some big companies who will fund your research. So, if you are good at it, it's only a matter of time before something will click. But it was getting more competitive each year.
>
> (Appleby University)

For this interviewee, this highlights that research intensity was becoming more competitive in the UK.

> **Interviewee 3:**
> Massification in the UK – probably, because it comes down to quality versus quantity.
>
> (Beta University)

Larger class sizes and greater diversity was affecting this academic. The second highest UK challenge was stated as the impact on work life balance. Three academics came under this category:

Interviewee 9:

I was young and used to work late. Lots of hours working in the FE/HE sector. I taught about 6 subjects per week. It was a diverse range of subjects – business, a bit of IT, a bit of finance, some marketing etc.

(Beta University)

For this case, the interviewee was working in an FE/HE institution where the academic taught HND programs and professional qualifications.

4.9.2 Overseas – Greatest Challenge

The greater challenge faced by academics overseas was in teaching related areas such as coping with stress in the classroom due to the immaturity levels of the students, relevancy of the curriculum or trying to get students to pass in a British University system:

Interviewee 2:

I think the greatest challenge was teaching too many courses in the first years alongside extreme stress in not being able to cope with the immaturity of Asian students.

(Appleby University)

This emphasis in this particular case that workload in their UAE role is perceived as greater compared to their previous UK experience and that immaturity can be disturbing for some academics in handling these students.

Interviewee 10:

I was thinking of the analogy the other day. The greatest challenge is to get these students through the programme. You know, trying to get non-British students through a very British academic programme.

(Appleby University)

This interviewee emphasised the challenge she faced to get students to a comparable standard given the lower entry standards at the overseas branch campus.

Interviewee 3:

Biggest challenge, again the relevancy of teaching and learning related to the local culture.

(Beta University)

For this interviewee, the challenge initially was in finding relevant local examples to help explain concepts in the classroom.

Three categories were joint second highest (with three of the academics selecting each category) – research, settling in and work-life balance. Three of the interviewees suggested that the lack of research momentum or dearth of funding income in the UAE was perceived as a real challenge in achieving career promotion or producing publications. This also can to be linked to section 4.8 when the findings highlight the difficulty in moving back to the UK as research was of great significance to recruitment into a good UK HE institution – three of the interviewees suggested that work-life balance caused them the greatest challenge in the UAE:

Interviewee 9:

Honestly, when I moved here, it was myself on my own. No wife or children, that wasn't too bad but the greatest challenge now is time management and sleep management really. I've got a young family and 6:00am latest every morning. If I'm working the night before to 9:30pm this can be tricky. As a Programme Coordinator, it's up to me to get staff, get the part-timers to do the teaching while I concentrate on running the program and teaching ... this is the greatest challenge and it is work-life!

(Beta University)

Full-time and part-time Masters Students are taught during the evenings. For this interviewee, he has to teach three evenings per week alongside day classes and office hours for students.

> **Interviewee 1:**
> Probably the biggest challenge here is not to let work take over your life. Given my professional role and all other bits and pieces that you have to do can be consuming. It is trying to find the balance, which is tremendously difficult here. The job takes more time than you can give.
>
> (Appleby University)

This interviewee wanted to do research but had no time available to do so which caused her frustration, as she wanted to return back to the UK HE sector. Three of the interviewees said that settling down into the overseas appointment was highly stressful and challenging which mirrors and substantiates the findings of the Richardson (2000) study of thirty expatriate academics:

> **Interviewee 8:**
> I think it was the first two months for me settling here. It was just facing the cliff as if there was nowhere else to go. So you go back to your hotel, you feel left out. You come to work, you meet new people all the time and partly one of those things on its own would be acceptable but all of them happening at once. I found the first 2 months really challenging.
>
> (Appleby University)

This quote highlights that loneliness can be a negative experience in the initial stages of the overseas position.

> **Interviewee 7:**
> I think it would be just getting the family tuned to the overseas experience more than anything else.
>
> (Beta University)

This quote certainly shows the major impact if the family is unsettled and can affect the work role of the academic.

4.9.3 Greatest Challenge – UAE or UK?

When asked to what extent was the challenge greater in the UAE or the UK, nine out of fourteen interviewees perceived that the UAE challenge to be greater; five of the interviewees stated that the greater challenge of the two remained in their UK experience. When breaking the data down, settling down at the beginning of the overseas position proved to be the greatest challenge for the UK expatriate academics followed by lack of research and work-life balance jointly. Four of the five interviewees stated that their UK challenge was the greater of the two and suggested that this was linked to the neo-liberalism forces that had taken place in the UK HE sector. The next section provides a brief summary of the major findings.

4.10 Conclusion

The key motive for working abroad has remained the same for over fifteen years since Richardson (2000) conducted her research into the motives and reasons for expatriate academics moving abroad. New categories have since come alongside such as those moving from the FE/HE sector to move into HE institutions abroad to those who were teaching initially part-time in a UK University or academics coming with their spouses. The background of the interviewees predominantly comes from a teaching-focused University. It is not common for researchers to move to an overseas campus, as it would be negative to their future career or promotion prospects.

Of particular concern is the theme of settling down at the beginning, induction and lack of mentoring support provided by the branch campuses. Given that this was cited as the highest category in their challenges this of great concern for both retention and helping expatriate academics settle into their roles more smoothly. More can be done by the branch campus to ensure that greater attention is spent on relocation support, on training and mentoring support. It was seen from two of the interviewee comments that multinational businesses are more supportive in this area. The lack of maturity level of students coupled with students who practiced rote learning presented several challenges to both new and experienced academics. These academics were used to teaching students in critical thinking in the UK and students tended to be more mature. The findings also highlight the various types of curriculum and assessment strategies practised at the three British Universities where the research was conducted.

These academics voiced criticism at the extreme end where a uniform curriculum (using the same teaching materials) and assessments were employed. Whereas those academics in this study that developed their own materials and assessments preferred this activity as it was more tailored to student learning and the cultural environment where they taught. This study identified that there is a difference (for those who taught previously at UK Universities) when it comes to allocation of modules that the academic teaches according to the respondents in this study. In the UK, academics teach to their specialist area at Universities. In an FE/HE environment academics would teach subjects not in their specialism. In the UAE branch campuses, it was found that expatriate academics would be allocated modules to teach that were sometimes not in their subject area, causing them anxiety and stress.

Minimal research is undertaken at the three British Universities in the UAE. There are several reasons for the lack of research such as limited funding available in the UAE but more obvious is the fact that these Universities operate in the private sector and any research work is seen as an additional expense reducing their profits or surpluses. Lack of research minimises the chances of returning to a high-ranking University and can affect their chances of returning back to the UK HE sector.

Administration appears to be more demanding for the academic working in an overseas branch campus. There are two factors contributing to this. Firstly, the administrative support tends to be poorly resourced compared to their UK counterparts according to the respondents in this study. Secondly, there is less infrastructural support in place to support students in counselling, academic enhancement or library specialisation etc. In one of the British Universities more infrastructural resources were provided. However, it did make a difference in reducing the workload for these academics.

Using and applying the Framework of Five Essential Elements of Academic Work (Gappa et al 2007), one clearly sees that professional growth, autonomy and employment equity is considerably less than that of academics working in the UK HE sector. More opportunities are available to UK academics for individual personal development and opportunities to attend conferences or to conduct PhD supervision.

They can still develop their own materials albeit of prescribed learning outcomes in contrast to many of the academics interviewed in this study that did not have this autonomy. Research is seen as pivotal to the academic career in the UK. Given the lack of research undertaken, this lowers the opportunities of academics to move back to the UK or gain career advancement via publications. Collegiality and flexibility appear to be similar to the UK academic's role although in the UK academics have greater decision-making power to influence operations based on the findings from this study.

Effective relationship building is essential to ensure smooth handling of operations exists between both campuses. A number of tactics have helped to develop relationship building such as personal one-to-one meetings which helps build rapport and trust. The majority of academics have recognised this and made every effort to make their relationships matter with their counterparts. However, there were several accounts of negative experiences of some interviewees where the relationship was poor or counterparts were too busy themselves. Skype was a popular communication method alongside the use of telephone and emails. However, it is difficult to clearly hear all committee members in Skype conference calls.

The greatest UK challenges perceived by the interviewees were the neo-liberalism forces that have been impacting the UK HE sector. For the greatest challenge overseas, the largest category was teaching followed jointly by work-life balance, lack of research and settling-in. Overseas challenges are perceived by expatriate academics to have been more demanding overall. Settling in at the beginning of the overseas appointment was the greatest challenge faced by academics. This finding echoes similar trends reviewed in the literature but it has been helpful to prioritise which challenge has been most impactful on expatriate academics.

The next Chapter provides discussion on these findings and draw together implications from the study.

Chapter 5

DISCUSSION AND IMPLICATIONS

Chapter Four provided the major findings of this research study based in the UAE private HE sector. In this Chapter, I provide discussion of these findings and their implications linking them to original research investigation. In Section 5.1, I firstly discusses the broader theme that British branch campuses (based in the UAE) are teaching-led institutions in practice and broadly resemble FE/HE colleges which are based in the UK. Given the background of the interviewees from this field study and the apparent lack of research being conducted at these branch campuses this has serious implications for both the branch campus and those academics seeking to return to the UK HE sector. The majority of academics working at these branch campuses have perceived their chances to return to the UK HE sector have been lowered due to their lack of publications and research output. A previous research study indicated that the UK HE sector does not value international experience unlike the USA and Australia, which see these experiences as a valuable skill set in enhancing their institutions (Richardson and Zikic, 2007). The researcher argues in this section that branch campuses must place more emphasis on research as it improves the learning and teaching experience and upholds and protects the UK University brand globally. Research has particular implications for improving dissertation support and enhances teaching in the classroom.

Section 5.2 provides discussion and implications for addressing the lack of support mechanisms in place for newly arriving academics to the UAE. This was the greatest challenge identified by the interviewees in the study and has caused stress, culture shock and anxiety to themselves (or to their immediate family members). The support for newly arriving academics and settling in, induction and lack of formalised mentoring systems proved to be inadequate as per the experiences of the majority of interviewees in this study. In this section, I include training support for pedagogy which was the highest overall challenge category perceived by the interviewees for the greatest overseas challenge (please refer to Table 4.1 in Chapter Four). Both are seen as integral to supporting the academic in their role. Induction support is also recommended for all part-time academics to ensure the consistency of approach in maintaining academic standards.

In section 5.3, the researcher addresses the five essential components of academic work identified in the Gappa et al (2007) Framework. In this study, the evidence shows that in four of the five core elements of the framework need to be addressed if respect is to be upheld for the academic. The study (conducted in UAE private sector Universities) is compared to the Chapman et al (2014) study using the same framework applied to UAE public and semi-public Universities. Many similarities co-exist at both private and public sector Universities in the two studies. I shall address each of these core areas and provide some recommendations to help improve academic conditions of those academics working in the UAE HE sector.

In section 5.4, I discuss how inadequate resourcing in both services and administrative support has affected the role of the expatriate increasing their workload and ultimately has a negative effect on work-life balance. It is recommended that employing more full-time academics would significantly reduce workload on existing full-time academic staff. Several problems have been identified on employing too heavy an importance on the employment of part-time adjunct faculty. Improving the infrastructural support at the branch campuses provides a better overall student experience and will help academics to improve their work-life balance. The conclusions of this Chapter are presented in Section 5.5. Many of the points link together and are integral to the role of the expatriate academics.

5.1 Drawbacks of working abroad

The next section discusses the implications of moving abroad for the expatriate academic and their future career aspirations. In Chapter

Four, it was revealed that the primary motive for moving abroad to work in transnational Higher Education was largely motivated by the 'adventure seeking' profile of the academic. Several new categories had formed since Richardson's (2000) research was published on motives and careers of academics in transnational Higher Education. The background of the interviewees' UK HE experiences originated largely from teaching Universities and four came from FE/HE institutions. Few researchers tended to move abroad as it was not beneficial to their future career prospects (i.e. research output has been the main factor contributing to career promotion) (Fielden and Gillard, 2011). The findings from Chapter Four also highlighted the fact that the overall perception of the majority of academics in this study perceived that it would be far more difficult to move back to the UK HE sector. One of the main reasons for this was lack of research and publications. Some felt that they could go back but at a lower position compared to that position they originally had before leaving their UK University. A few interviewees stated that they might find a job in a niche University that specialised predominantly in teaching to the international student market.

Another reason why it would be difficult to move back to the UK HE sector was the situational circumstances in which the academics work in. The three British branch campuses in this study are teaching institutions whose students tend to have lower entry standards than to their UK campuses. In addition, due to the maturity levels of students and the fact that resources are not on par with their UK home-based University campus – they resemble FE/HE institutions in practice. Lim's (2010) research confirms that in practice, Universities are less likely to make investments in their overseas campus infrastructure due to profit motivation. The recent QAA Overseas Transnational Review that took place in 2014 also confirms finding - resourcing and infrastructure at UAE branch campuses are not on par with home campuses. The lack of research and relatively few PhD student supervisions being conducted takes away an important ingredient in University life. De Meyer (2012) has argued for global research and teaching to form the basis of a successful overseas institution and that to maintain the University brand, it is essential to uphold this important element of the academic role. Hughes (2011) study argues that there is a perception at British Universities that academics view their branch campus counterpart's role inferior to their role at the main branch. The study reveals that overseas providers do not embrace quality assurance and enhancement due to underinvestment in staffing, student resourcing and facilities as mentioned earlier in the literature. The research findings of this study reveal that there are limited opportunities to become involved in the UK home campus governance structures or restrictions for expatriate academics to develop module materials for both home and overseas operations or to be involved in curriculum design. The QAA Transnational Review of HE in the UAE (2014) also confirms this as missing the 'DNA' of British Higher Education that is essential to a British University Degree (similar findings are made by Salt and Wood 2014). Not only is the lack of research affecting expatriate careers, there is the perception that working overseas is not valuable to the UK academic professional unlike the value placed by the USA or Australian Higher Education systems (Richardson and Zikic, 2007). The UK HERA system of promotion does not embrace international experience for career promotion.

The implication of these findings is that UK Universities should raise their level of scrutiny over their overseas branch campuses to ensure that their brand is protected both globally and in the UAE. This would require branch campuses to provide greater investment of resources for supporting students and in stimulating a research culture. For the University, this enhances their reputation in the global market place. For the academic, it would make an overseas appointment appear a much more attractive work environment for research-intensive academics. It would be of tremendous benefit for expatriate academics to be able to return to the UK HE sector. If Universities are to adapt these recommendations, they must enforce franchisees to undertake this expense as part of their contractual franchise agreement and obligations. For the branch campus, it would require the reduction of teaching hours to allow academics more time to spend on their research and develop a research culture at the branch campus. The findings indicate that workload is one of the causes that academics have spent very limited time to conduct research. Small grants should be made available for the branch campus to enable research to be kick-started given the scarcity of research funds available in the UAE. The home campus should jointly help expatriate academics at the branches to become fully involved in their research groups to help achieve and build up research culture and support collaboration. There are two other reasons why research is important and fundamental for University branch campuses. Firstly, conducting research helps academics in teaching both undergraduate and Masters levels by keeping themselves up-to-date in their subject area and it also enhances more meaningful dissertation supervision and guidance. As International Branch Campuses expand their portfolio of postgraduate programmes this is becoming an essential element of enhancing learning and teaching. The second reason why research is important to academics working at branch campuses is that it is an expectation of the academic role itself. If academics teach standardised courses then they are most likely to move elsewhere if salary packages are higher than their current packages. Research helps to reduce academic churn and this is a core element of the academic professional role itself. As Gappa et al (2007) purport that failure to provide these essential entitlements lead to academic turnover, apathy, lower productivity and 'not going that extra mile'. They argue that there are costs involved that are associated with the failure to provide basic entitlements and with them not in place, academic staff will not value any benefits. The findings of this research study indicate negative feelings amongst several academics in not been able to conduct research comparing their experiences to academics working in the UK HE sector.

5.2 The need to support newly arriving academics and part-time faculty

This section discusses the implications of branch campuses not supporting newly arriving academics with their families and not providing a formalised induction programme and mentoring support system. If addressed and put in place, this eases the transformation of settling into their roles more smoothly, reducing stress and anxiety and leading to enhanced work performance across the institution.

In Chapter Four, the interviewees in this study answered that teaching overseas students was the greatest challenge that they faced in their work. A similar finding was provided in Clarke's (2013) study of expatriate academics, which highlighted the problems of teaching international students. When asked to compare between the UK experience and overseas experience in this study, settling-in was found to be the greatest impact challenge (refer to Table 4.1, Chapter Four). The findings of the study indicated that there was limited or no assistance provided in the support for academics (and their families) in settling-in. Numerous studies (Richardson and McKenna 2002; Ward et al 2001; Pyvis and Chapman 2005) confirm this as a major issue in transnational higher education and will affect the lives of overseas academics causing anxiety, stress and culture shock. Several challenges were cited in this study from finding accommodation, difficulty in opening a bank account, challenges in finding schools for the family, arranging transport; problems experienced in teaching to coping with a new cultural environment. In the two cases of those academics who came on their spouse's visa to the UAE the transition of settling in was much smoother in contrast to those academics who faced difficulties when joining their respective UAE Universities. Multinational organisations provide care and attention in relocating employees and their family members. They recognise the need to ensure that their employees are looked after in order to make their transition into their new country as smooth as possible (Richardson and Zikic, 2007). Branch campuses should also provide this support, as it would reduce stress, culture shock and anxiety for many newly arriving academics. For the organisation, it will enhance their reputation of being a responsible employer and help build employee commitment and strengthen loyalty. It would contribute to improving staff retention by helping towards keeping academics stay longer at their institution.

This study has highlighted that newly arriving academics struggle in the classroom with handling immature students and in adapting their teaching pedagogy given that the learning styles of students differ to UK students. It takes some time for academics to adjust and learn how to cope with these challenges. Employing an experienced Public Relations Officer to support both work and personal matters are essential for supporting the smooth arrival of the newly appointed academic into the country. Richardson and Zikic (2007) have also made this recommendation in their research study of expatriate academics (based on fifteen academics working in Singapore). Two studies conducted by Dunn and Wallace (2006) and Gribble and Ziguras (2003) also found that support and pre-departure training to be minimal in overseas campuses. Schermerhorn (1999) has suggested that overseas branches support families, as it can be a challenging experience if not handled well. This research study highlights the need to develop a formalised induction training and mentoring support for newly arriving academics and for part-time faculty to receive training and support in awareness of policies, procedures and marking. The difficulties in teaching overseas students have proven a challenge even for the most experienced of academics in their first year of teaching. Fox (1983) refers to this as a 'mismatch' by the teacher and the students in the classroom. He posits, "in this case it is the students who view the teaching and learning process as a transfer of knowledge. They will expect well-structured lectures that leave them with a set of comprehensive notes, which they can learn and later produce in an examination. Such students will be impatient with any attempts at introducing experiential learning such as projects, simulations and games. They will see such exercises as a waste of time because they know that the information transferred in such procedures can be transferred much more rapidly in lectures and duplicated notes" (p.160). This study's findings indicate the need to incorporate teaching pedagogy for multi-cultural students and teaching strategies to handle immature students in the classroom and provide cultural awareness to reduce culture shock. Austin and Chapman (2002) have also argued for the development of academics working overseas. These need to be built into induction programmes alongside formalised mentoring systems.

There is another reason why formalised induction and mentoring systems are important for branch campuses. This study has revealed that many academics of differing nationalities work in overseas branch campuses. A standardised approach is necessary to ensure that the British Higher Education system maintains academic standards. For example, in many countries higher education systems vary when it comes to marking bands. It is essential that part-time faculty attend induction-training programmes alongside full-time faculty. They also need to be part of the formalised mentoring system. UK Universities need to monitor via their quality enhancement units that formalised induction and mentoring systems are in place and are fully supported by the home campus. Similar findings were found in the recent QAA Transnational Audit of British Universities (2014) operating in the UAE that part-time academics received little or no induction training or support. One essential part of the induction training is to increase awareness of building effective relationships with counterparts at the home campus. A number of tactics have proved useful in helping improve more effective working relationships such as personal contact, building rapport with counterparts, use of Skype communication and regular phone calls to keep in contact. The benefits are several fold as trust and respect are formed between the home and branch campus. It also enhances positive perceptions of the branch campus (similar to the findings made by Smith 2009).

5.3 Lessons on building respect

This next section discusses the implications of the findings from the application of the chosen conceptual framework – the Five Essential Elements Framework (Gappa et al, 2007). There are several parallels from this study to those made to the UAE study of thirty-seven UAE expatriate academics working in the public and semi-public Universities (conducted by Chapman et al, 2014). Firstly, there were similar comparisons made in both studies on the curb on academic freedom particularly in the classroom. Academics had to be sensitive to country specific cultural sensitivity. However in terms of autonomy, there are substantial differences appearing between the two studies. In the public University sector there is full autonomy provided to the academic to develop programme materials and in setting assessments. The Chapman et al (2014) study suggests that academics were happy with their autonomy in the classroom. In this study, there was slight differences of approach when designing course materials and setting assessments for those interviewees who had to use standardised materials (with some contextualisation) or how they developed their own materials but applying the same assessments. In the case of setting their own materials and assessments it was evident that academics welcomed their autonomy just as in the public sector study whereas those who were teaching standardised materials felt negative about their loss of their autonomy.

In terms of collegiality, there were similarities in positive horizontal collegiality amongst staff found in both studies and they are comparable in the UK. However, it was more noticeable in this study that warm respect was present from top management although very limited input was made into decision-making that took place concerning governance at the main campus. The UAE QAA Transnational Review of Higher Education (2014) has made a recommendation for British Universities to involve their overseas academics in the decision making processes of their home-based Universities. This study indicated that more decision-making in operations took place by academics in the UK HE sector.

Both studies are similar in the lack of professional development opportunities made available. Research was also lacking in both studies at the public and private sector Universities. Chapman et al (2014) are critical that this would not lead to building world-class institutions. Given that research is limited at the overseas branch campuses employment equity does not favour those academics seeking to return back to the UK HE sector given that research output forms the basis for career advancement for UK academics. Chapman et al (2014) suggested that the three-year contracts posed a problem in that this did not develop long-term commitment or any potential to develop research at the public sector Universities. For interviewees in this study, they did not see their continuation or security of employment as a potential problem. There is a distinct difference between the studies.

When linking the core elements of the framework, it is apparent that respect provided for the overseas academic is not present in four elements to allow both the institution and the academics to fully benefit. The deskilling that academics experience in teaching other's materials can be overcome if overseas academics can participate and can be part of the institutional process to develop materials and in setting assessments. This can be very useful for creating a set of international materials. Overseas academics will be more knowledgeable when it comes to developing an international curriculum that could be taught across many overseas campuses. They have insight into the international context rather than being specific for UK students. Both the home and overseas campus would benefit from such an international approach being delivered. As we have seen from this study, academics who deliver their own materials feel that they have regained their autonomy whereas in the opposite extreme Schapper and Mayson (2004) cite 'rob' the academic of 'intellectual stimulation' and engagement.

Greater resource needs to be invested by the branch campus in terms of providing professional development that is tailored and focused on individual needs. This would help improve the performance of the institution and enhance their reputation as a responsible and committed employer. This needs to be integral to the performance appraisal system conducted at these institutions. It is noticeable that in all three British branch campuses that the performance appraisal system has only been recently adopted whereas they have been in existence in the UK HE sector for over a decade.

It is important that overseas academics become involved in the governance of the University decision-making process. For the branch campus, this helps to develop vertical collegiality with the home campus. For the home campus, this acknowledges respect for their overseas branch campuses. This avoids and minimises the 'parent' versus 'child' relationship (Smith, 2009). In Section 5.1, I recommended that branch campuses should focus and build upon research. If this were actioned, it would improve employment equity and raise levels of respect for academics. The next section discusses increased workload faced by overseas academics.

5.4 Increased Workload

Chapter Four identified that academics often face increased workload when there is a poor level of resource in place at the branch campus due to inadequate administration support levels, poor resourcing levels in the academic enhancement units and no counselling or career units in place. This study found that in two out of the three cases investigated, this was inappropriate causing increased workload and on occasions stress in coping with student problems of a non-academic nature. In the other case, a more advanced level of support services was in place, which did lead to a positive effect on the workload of the academic staff.

Given the lower entry levels and immaturity of students identified in the study, it is essential to provide these services to students. It is dangerous for academics to become involved in personal counselling when they are not qualified. They are not qualified to provide effective careers advice and the ownership is on the branch campus as a responsible employer to provide these as they do at the home campus. Similar findings and recommendations were identified in the recent QAA UAE Transnational Review of Higher Education (2014). Academic support can be an effective means to improving and enhancing the student learning experience at Universities. Adequate and qualified administrator resources are also important to supporting the function and nature of academic work. This was particularly poor at both Appleby University and Charleston University causing many problems and extra duties amongst their interviewees. Additional extra duties such as attending open days each month and making student application decisions were expected of academic staff despite an admissions team in place. The academics in this study suggested that they spent considerably more time on marketing than what they experienced in their UK positions.

From the study findings, it was revealed that several of the interviewees had to teach some subjects which were not in their specialism. From a quality standpoint, this practice may affect the learning experiences of students taking these modules and causes stress and anxiety to the academic who teaches them. UK home based Universities should be monitoring teaching allocations at their branch campuses to ensure that this practice is stopped. It can lead to a potential risk to their brand and reputation. Branch campuses need to respect the professional role of the academic and owe a duty of care when allocating teaching modules. It not only strengthens their reputation in the market but also reduces stress and stops academics being placed in difficult and uncomfortable positions. To-date, no study has highlighted this finding in the transnational higher education literature. This study also confirms findings to those made by the UAE QAA review of transnational Higher Education in that the employment of part-time adjunct faculty at the branch campuses was particularly high and could affect quality. Part-time faculty are paid an-hourly rate and are not given a visa permit or access to privileges such as holiday pay, housing allowances or severance pay. It was highlighted that interviewees in this study had to help answer student queries when the part-time faculty were off campus resulting in additional workload. Several of the interviewees in this study have also suggested that this affects students if part-time academics are not given office hours. Branch campuses need to review carefully the implications of using too high a ratio of part-time academics, as it does not contribute to developing enhancement of the overall student learning experience. Several of the interviewees revealed that their part-time academic colleagues were teaching across several Universities with very heavy teaching loads (in some cases up to thirty hours per week contact time with students). One therefore questions the quality of teaching if inadequate time is not spent in preparing for classes. Another problem identified from this study was that part-time faculty teach across varying higher education systems which questions the variability in marking. Employing further full-time academic employments helps to address some of the issues identified and help contribute to raising the quality of the student learning experience.

Work-life balance was identified as a major issue for some of the interviewees in this study. Employers have a duty of care to provide a work-place environment where employees are given the opportunity to be productive and have the right resources in place to conduct their role. Addressing these resource deficiencies will have a very positive effect on the work-life balance of the overseas academic and allow them to be on par with their UK counterparts. For the overseas students, this study has revealed that students receive a better overall learning experience when these are in place.

5.5 Conclusions

Chapter Four showed that the interviewees perceived working overseas as significantly more challenging compared to their experiences of working in the UK HE sector. Those who did suggest that the UK challenge was greater suggested that they resulted from the impact of neo-liberal forces as discussed in the literature review.

This Chapter has suggested several areas to improve the work environment and role of the academic working overseas that would raise the UK University brand and improve the overall student learning experience. Involving overseas academics in the decision-making processes at the home campus will play a pivotal role to improving relationships and acknowledgement of their contribution to transnational higher education. Overseas academics have knowledge and understanding of the international curriculum and should become more involved in developing the international curriculum, course materials and assessments. This would also prevent deskilling of the academic role. Improving the infrastructural support for students will help overseas academics in their academic role and improve the student experience. Initiatives to increase the investment into research at branch campuses are fundamental to ensuring that the UK University brand is not diluted but enhanced. Research has an important role to play in improving teaching and learning and is key for academic promotion in the UK. It would raise the chances for overseas academics to return back to the UK HE sector. Branch campuses should make greater investment and support for the professional development of the academic. In addition, branch campuses need to improve the work-life balance of their academic staff, as it will help improve retention and quality of life. The greatest challenge faced by overseas academics in this study was the issues faced in settling-in and adjusting and adapting teaching pedagogy. It was argued in section 5.2 that greater help and support is required to ensure the smooth arrival of the academic (and their families) in settling-in. A formal induction programme that incorporates cultural awareness, developing effective relationships with counterparts, teaching pedagogy, handling immature students alongside University policies and procedures and an introduction to the UAE and library are essential. It is also recommended that all newly arriving faculty be assigned to an experienced member of staff in a formal mentoring system.

In the next Chapter, conclusions are drawn from those arising from the findings, analysis and discussion in Chapters Four and Five. The researcher reviews the research question, sub-questions and re-visits the literature presented in Chapter Two. Further areas of study will be identified for future research.

Chapter Six

CONCLUSION - CONCLUDING REMARKS AND PERSONAL INSIGHTS

6.1 Introduction

This research study has investigated the role of expatriate academics who work in the UAE private HE sector. A study was conducted capturing interviews of fourteen British expatriate academics. This Chapter is organised as follows: In section 6.2, the researcher returns to his original research question and provides a summative account and explanation of key findings, recommendations and significance of this research study. Section 6.3 discusses future research studies that could be applied from this study.

6.2 Review of Research Questions

The primary research question for this research study was as follows:

How does the overseas conditions and environment affect the professional role of the British expatriate academic?

For academics working in the UAE, there are a number of key differences in which the role varies in relation to the role in the UK HE sector. This research revealed that academic workload is higher than in the UK HE sector and agrees with previous research (Macdonald 2006; Richardson and McKenna 2002; Pyvis 2011; and Dobos 2011). This has implications that increase stress and affects teaching quality, as academics need adequate time in preparing for classes and assessing students. There is less opportunity for personal development and research is not prioritised at private sector universities given the strong emphasis placed upon teaching. This finding agrees with research already undertaken (Macdonald 2006; Barry et al 2003; Richardson and Zikic 2007; Fielden and Gillard 2011). The administration workload appears to be higher than it was in their UK academic experiences largely as a result of constrained resources in supporting the academic community. This is an important finding as it was difficult to see if there were similarities or differences in the literature review (please refer to the summary table of the literature in Chapter Two). Macdonald (2006) has indicated that greater administration input leads to increased stress in the role.

Academics tended to have less input on decision-making than their counterparts in the UK. The study also indicated that teaching was more challenging than it was in their experience of teaching in the UK, which was due to the student maturity levels, and customisation to students coming from a rote learning background. Previous research (Lane 2011a; Teekens 2003; Crose 2011; Woodhouse and Stella 2008; Cross and Burdett 2012; Dunn and Wallace 2006; and Gabb 2006) agrees with this finding. Where standardised teaching content and materials were used across campuses, this presented these academics with the sense of deskilling their role. It caused difficulties in teaching delivery for both the academic and students alike. This finding is similar to those claims made by Macdonald (2006) and Dobos (2011).

In Chapter Two, I described the neoliberal impacts that have affected the role of the UK academic over the past five decades. Despite these impacts, the majority of academics in this study suggest that working in transnational higher education is perceived to be more challenging than working in the UK HE sector. The findings of this study agree with the literature presented in Chapter Two that overseas academics face a number of challenges that affects their professional role. This study has gone one step further in prioritising which of the challenges has been the greatest impact on the academic working overseas. The researcher has established that settling in and teaching to multi-cultural students is recognised to be the greatest of challenges affecting expatriate academics. Several recommendations have therefore been put forward in Chapter Five to address these major factors such as support for moving to the new country, developing a formalised induction programme to include cultural, training supporting teaching pedagogy and adopting formalised mentoring systems. I argue in Section 6.3 for further research in other countries to confirm these new research findings. Previous research agrees with findings on lack of induction and preparation for new academics. The following researchers confirm that there is lack of induction in coping with pedagogical strategies to manage with cross-cultural teaching and adjusting with cultural dimensions (Schermerhorn 1999; Richardson and McKenna 2002; Chapman and Austin 2002; Bodycott and Walker 2000; Woodhouse and Stella 2008; and Dunn and Wallace 2006). The studies conducted by Schermerhorn (1999), Richardson and McKenna (2002), and Richardson and Zikic (2007) confirm with my findings that there are issues with schooling, housing and obtaining medical and visa clearances. The findings also indicated that academics could be lonely and develop feelings of alienation in settling-in. These are similar to previous research findings made by Schermerhorn (1999), Gopal (2011) and Lane (2011a).

Other contributions from this research include the problems in marking by part-time adjunct faculty at the three British Universities where I conducted research. It was recognised from the interviews that there were many examples of part-time faculty members teaching across a number of Universities. Different grading systems employed at these Universities (e.g. American, British, Indian, and Australian etc.) lead to instances of grade inflation/deflation. In Chapter Five, the researcher has recommended that all part-time faculty members attend induction training alongside full-time faculty to ensure that academic standards are in place.

The third new contribution to academic knowledge reveals that academics who come to work overseas have tended to come from UK teaching-focused Universities or FE/HE Colleges. The discussion in Chapter Five argued that this made it difficult for academics to return back to the UK HE sector for a number of reasons. Richardson and Zikic (2007) indicated that normally expatriate academics had no job to go back to in the UK referring this to "the dark side" of working overseas. In the Richardson (2000) study, there was a sense of positivism, that the 'international experience' would be an asset for returning back to the UK HE sector. In this study (fifteen years later), there was a sense of negative feelings amongst the majority of interviewees that their international experience was perceived as a liability in returning back to the UK HE sector. Thirteen of the fourteen interviewees all indicated that it would be more difficult to return to the UK HE sector.

Linking to this discussion, the researcher argues in Chapter Five that lack of research in the three private sector Universities has serious implications for the quality of dissertation supervision and teaching at Masters level. How do academics keep themselves up-to-date if research is not conducted? If overseas branches are to be considered a UK equivalent qualification, they must support research informed teaching. Simply regurgitating another academic's teaching materials does not enhance the quality of the student learning experience. The researcher puts forward recommendations for overseas branch campuses to increase research activity as it would enhance the student learning experience as well as provide the overseas academic community with the opportunity to bring research into their teaching and improve the level of dissertation supervision and Masters teaching. The application of the Framework of Essential Elements (Gappa et al, 2007) helped me to inform and develop several of the recommendations to improve 'respect' for the overseas academic professional role and enhance the development of the branch campus. As it currently stands, UK academics have greater autonomy, more influence in making operational decisions, improved employment equity and opportunities for professional growth compared to overseas academics as the findings in this study reflect.

6.3 Future Research Studies in other Countries

The research design applied for this study allows for future studies to be conducted in other counties where transnational higher education exists. By using an identical research design and applying the same semi-structured questionnaire this research study can be replicated elsewhere. Similar research studies would be helpful for comparison purposes. Do expatriate academics face similar challenges in these countries? Are they facing similar findings of challenges of settling in and in coping with teaching pedagogy? What is the greatest challenge at home and in the host country?

Further research is required into teaching pedagogy in transnational higher education. This is an essential area as many of the interviewees in this study struggled to cope in teaching students and they prioritised this as one of their greatest challenges. Very limited research has been produced in this field and it would be of particular benefit to academics working in transnational higher education and would be helpful in enhancing student learning. Key research questions concerts the most effective pedagogy to use in enhancing student learning and how to cope with the maturity levels of students? What is the best method to approach assessment feedback? A qualitative approach using focus groups, semi-structure interviews and teaching observations would be the most appropriate research methods to apply.

Appendices

Appendix One

Person Attributes

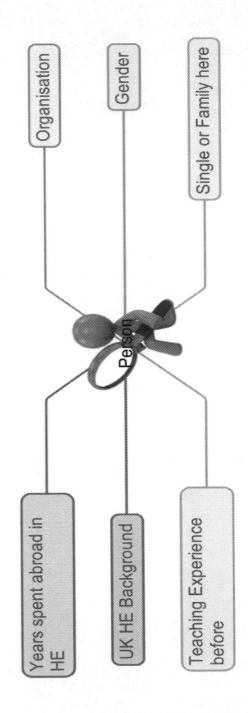

Person Name	sex	Years abroad	Single or famil...	UK HE Background	Teaching Experience before moving abroad
Transcrip...	Female	One to Two Years	Family	FE/HE College	five years and more
Transcrip...	Male	Five Years and more	Family	HE Teaching	five years and more
Transcrip...	Male	Five Years and more	Family	HE Teaching	five years and more
Transcrip...	Male	Five Years and more	Single	FE/HE College	five years and more
Transcrip...	Male	Five Years and more	Family	FE/HE College	five years and more
Transcrip...	Male	Two to Five Years	Family	HE Teaching	five years and more
Transcrip...	Male	Five Years and more	Family	FE/HE College	five years and more
Transcrip...	Male	One to Two Years	Single	HE Teaching	five years and more
Transcrip...	Male	Two to Five Years	Family	HE Teaching	five years and more
Transcrip...	Female	Five Years and more	Single	HE Teaching	five years and more
Interview...	Female	Five Years and more	Single	HE Teaching	five years and more
Meeting...	Female	Two to Five Years	Family	HE Research &...	five years and more
Transcrip...	Male	One to Two Years	Single	HE Teaching	two to five years
Transcrip...	Male	One to Two Years	Family	HE Teaching	five years and more

Appendix Two

Study of British Expatriate Academics

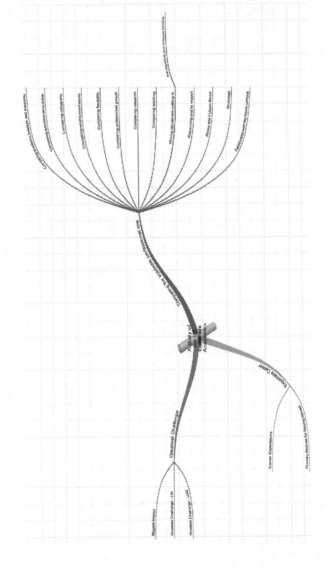

Appendix Three

Semi-Structured Interview Questions

Semi-structured Interview Questionnaire

Name:	
University:	

| Theme 1: |
| Motives for working overseas |

Question One:
What were your primary motives for working overseas?

Question Two:
Were you previously working in an HE sector in which you were research active or based upon a teaching only employment?

Question Three:
How long have you been working in the UAE? Any previous overseas HE experience?

Theme 2:
Moving abroad and settling in

Question Four:
What personal challenges did you (and your immediate family) face in moving abroad and settling in? Did you face any form of culture shock? Does it still exist?

Question Five:
Did you receive any pre-departure training or training when you joined the campus?

Theme 3:
Comparing teaching overseas to the UK

Question Six:
What have you found to be the key differences in comparing your teaching experience overseas to your experience of teaching in the UK?

Question Seven:
How do you feel about delivering a standardised curriculum and assessment strategy? To what extent does the curriculum and assessment tailor to the needs of your students?

Question Eight:
Have you faced any stress in your classes? If so, what were the causes?

Question Nine:
How have you coped with student interaction? (Both inside and outside the class)

> **Theme 4:**
> **Comparing research overseas to the UK**

Question Ten:

How does research differ here to the UK? What are the barriers and constraints to undertaking research?

Question Eleven:

What implications does research have for you and to your institution? How does it affect your future career aspirations?

> **Theme 5**
> **Comparing administrative duties to the UK**

Question Twelve:

How do your administrative duties compare to the UK?

> **Theme 6**
> **Relationships with the home campus**

Question Thirteen:

How would you describe your relationship with your colleagues at the home campus? How does time, distance and communication mediums play a role in this relationship? What tactics have been used in addressing them?

Theme 7
Comparability of the academic professional role applying the Framework of Essential Elements

---

Question Fourteen:
How would you describe collegiality in your workplace and how does it compare to your experience of working in the UK HE sector?

Question Fifteen:
How would you describe academic freedom and autonomy in your workplace and how does it compare to your experience of working in the UK HE sector?

Question Sixteen:
How would you describe professional growth in your workplace and how does it compare to your experience of working in the UK HE sector?

Question Seventeen:
How would you describe flexibility in your work place and how does this compare to your experience of working in the UK HE sector?

Question Eighteen:
How does employment equity here compare to your experience of working in the UK HE sector?

Theme 8
Resourcing and its impact on the role of the expatriate academic

---

Question Nineteen:
The UK HE sector have better resources for students. How does resourcing affect your role in this campus?

Question Twenty:
What are the implications of using part-timers for your role? Is this comparable to the UK experience?

Theme 9
Career expectations and future plans to move back to the UK or another overseas country

---

Question Twenty-One:
Having moved overseas how do you think your career expectations compare to those if you had of remained in the UK?

Question Twenty-Two:
Would you think it easy or difficult in returning back to the UK HE sector?

Theme 10
Greatest challenge affecting expatriate academics

Question Twenty-Three:
What is your greatest of all challenges facing you in your role? What was your greatest challenge that you faced in your previous role whilst in the UK HE sector?

Appendix Four

UK Challenge versus UAE Challenge – which is the greatest challenge?

Interviewee No.	UK Challenge	UAE Challenge	Greatest Challenge
1	Teaching Chinese students.	Work-life balance.	UAE Work-life balance
2	Stress of moving from University to University.	Too many courses + stress at beginning of job due to student interaction.	UAE Too many courses + student interaction
11	Balancing full-time job + part-time teaching.	Workload at the beginning.	UAE Workload
12	Making things viable as income was getting harder to meet.	Soft side – dealing and coping with students.	UK Making things viable
9	Doing too many courses and at a diverse range in the FE/HE environment.	Work-life balance.	UK Too many courses of a diverse range
10	Trying to get research started. Highly competitive.	Getting students through the British programme.	UK Research
8	Nervous about teaching part-time to begin with.	Settling in – Personal. 2 months settling in to work as new.	UAE Settling in
7	At the beginning of teaching.	Settling in family.	Abroad Settling in family

6	Getting research going.	Getting research moving.	UK Getting research moving
4	Research funding getting harder.	Research – lack of funding.	UAE Research
3	Massification –quality vs quantity.	Relevance of teaching and learning to the local culture.	UK Massification –quality vs quantity
5	Balancing time as too many aspects to the role of PM.	Setting in + personal emotional journey.	UAE Setting in + personal emotional journey
14	Bureaucracy	Working in the semi-public university – a very unpleasant experience.	UAE University – public sector.
13	Government interventions – reduction in freedom + autonomy + prescription.	Lack of research – too much teaching.	UAE Research – lack of.

Appendix Five

Summary of Issues and Challenges for academics working in transnational higher education

Theme	Issue / Challenge	Implications	Source
Pre-joining the overseas campus	Lack of induction and preparation.	Unaware of pedagogical strategies to cope in the cross-cultural teaching and outside of the work environment.	Richardson and McKenna (2002); Schermerhorn (1999); Chapman and Austin (2002); Bodycott and Walker (2000); Dunn and Wallace (2012); Woodhouse and Stella (2008);
	Culture 'shock' (academic and/or family)	Leads to stress and alienation due to lack of inter-cultural training.	Lane (2011); Schermerhorn (1999); Bodycott and Walker (2000); Gopal (2011).
	Separation from family (who can remain in the home country)	Can lead to loneliness and alienation for both parties.	
	Schooling / housing / medical	Difficulties in settling into a new house or schooling of children.	Richardson and McKenna (2002); Schermerhorn (1999); Richardson and Zikic (2007)
	Resourcing of staff	Can lead to problems in time-tabling and operational running in teaching.	Lane (2011a)

The expatriate academic in post	More teaching hours / high workloads.	Can lead to stress and for students they can be taught for numerous subjects by the same tutor.	Macdonald (2006); Richardson and McKenna (2002); Pyvis (2008); Dobos (2011).
	Limited time for research.	Can reduce opportunity to move back to home country.	Macdonald (2006); Barry et al (2003); Richardson and Zikic (2007); Welch (1997); Fielden and Gillard (2011).
	Immature students / different schooling systems / spoon-feeding (pastoral care).	Can lead to stress and difficulty in teaching.	Lane (2011); Teekens (2003); Crose (2011); Devitta (2000); Verhoeven et al (2013); Woodhouse and Stella (2008); Crossman and Burdett (2012).
	Culture misunderstandings in teaching pedagogy.	Teaching to international or multi-cultural classes is highly demanding and stressful.	Dunn and Wallace (2012); Gabb (2006).
	Localisation/ globalisation of the curriculum.	Can lead to 'disillusive' students and difficulty in teaching.	Mahrous and Ahmed (2010); Crichton and Scarino (2007); Ermenc (2005); Woolf (2002); Sulkowski and Deakin (2009); Coleman (2003); Pyvis (2011); Schoorman (2000); Shams and Huisman (2012).
	More administrative input.	Stress in the job	Macdonald (2006)

	Lack of resources in research / networking opportunities and mentoring support / facilities / access to grants.	Can be a negative for the academic in his/ her career and moving back to the home country.	Macdonald (2006); Wilkins (2011).
	Commodification of the role.	Can cause friction between home and host campus.	Dobos (2011); Macdonald (2006); Altbach (2002).
	Lack of career structure and promotion.	Can lead to frustration.	Macdonald (2006);
	Lacking in resources.	Difficulty in teaching.	McBurnie and Chok (2006); Coleman (2003); Dunsworth (2008).
	Distance	Can lead to difficulties in communication.	Hughes (2011); Eldridge and Cranston (2009); Smith (2009); McBurnie (2000); Harding and Lammey (2011); Pyvis (2011).
Moving on	No position to go back home to.	A risk to the future career of the academic.	Richardson and Zikic (2007)

Bibliography

Allport, C. (2000). "Thinking globally, acting locally: Lifelong learning and the implications for university staff." Journal of Higher Education Policy and Management **22:**37-47.

Altbach, P.G. (2002). "Knowledge and education as international commodities." International Higher Education 28:2-5.

Altbach, P.G. (2002). "Resource Review: Perspectives on International Higher Education." Change **34**(3):29-31.

Altbach, P.G. (2003). The Decline of the Guru: the Academic Profession in Developing and Middle-Income Countries New York. Palgrave Publishers.

Altbach, P.G. (2009). "It's the Faculty, Stupid!! The Centrality of the Academic Profession." International Higher Education **55:**15-17.

Altbach, P.G. (2010). "Why branch campuses may be unsustainable." International Higher Education. **58:**1-2.

Altbach, P.G. and Knight, J. (2006). "The internationalization of higher education: motivations and realities." In The NEA 2006 Almanac of Higher Education (pp7-36). Washington, DC: National Education Association.

Altbach, P.G. and Knight, J. (2007). "The Internationalisation of Higher Education: Motivations and Realities." Journal of Studies in International Education **11:**290-305.

Anderson, G. (2008). "Mapping Academic Resistance in the Managerial University." Organisation **15**(2):251-270.

Anderson, R. (1998). "The 'Idea of a University' today." History and Policy.

http://www.historyandpolicy.org/papers/policy-paper-98.html (Last accessed: 5ᵗʰ March 2014)

Andrade, M.S. (2006). "International students in English-speaking universities: Adjustment factors." Journal of Research in International Education 5(2):131-154.

Austin, A.E. and Chapman, D.W. (2002). "Balancing Pressures, Forming Partnerships". In Chapman, D.W. and Austin, A.E. ed. Higher Education in the Developing World, Changing Contexts and Institutional Responses. Boston: Centre for International Higher Education and the Program in Higher Education, 253-261.

Austin, A.E., Chapman, D.W., Farah, S., Wilson, E. and Ridge, N. (2014). "Expatriate academic staff in the United Arab Emirates: the nature of their work experiences in higher education institutions." Higher Education 1-17.

Ball, S. S. (1998). "Big Policies/Small World: An Introduction to International Perspectives in Education Policy." Comparative Education, 34(2):119-130.

Barnett, R. (2000). Realising the University: in an age of supercomplexity. The Society for Research into Higher Education Open University Press, Buckingham.

Barry, J., Berg, E. and Chandler, J. (2003). "Managing intellectual labour in Sweden and England." Cross Cultural Management: An International Journal 10(3):3-22.

Beaty, L. (1998). "The professional development of teachers in higher education: Structures, methods and responsibilities." Innovations in Teaching and Education International 35(2):99-107.

Becher, T. and Trowler, P.R. (2011). Academic Tribes and Territories. The Society for Research into Higher Education. Open University Press, Buckingham.

Bell, E. and Bryman, A. (2007). "The Ethics of Management Research: An Exploratory Content Analysis." British Journal of Management **18**:63-77.

Bennell, P. and Pearce, T. (2003). "The internationalisation of higher education: exporting education to developing and transitional economies." International Journal of Educational Development **23**:215-232.

Biggs, J. (2003). Teaching for quality learning at University: What the student does. (2nd edition), Maidenhead, Berkshire: Open University Press.

Bitektine, A. (2008). "Prospective Case Study Design: Qualitative Method for Deduction Theory Testing." Organisational Research Methods **11**(1):168-180.

Black, J.S. and Stephens, G.K. (1989). "The influence of the spouse on American expatriate adjustment in the Pacific Rim overseas assignments." Journal of Management **15**:529–544.

Boden, R. and Epstein, D. (2006). "Managing the research imagination? Globalisation and research in higher education." Globalisation, Societies and Education **4**(2):223-236.

Bodycott, P. and Walker, A. (2000). "Teaching Abroad: Lessons learned about inter-cultural understanding for teachers in higher education." Teaching in Higher Education **5**(1):79-94.

Bott, E. (2010). "Favourites and others: reflexivity and the shaping of subjectivities and data in qualitative research." Qualitative Research **10**:159-173.

Bowen, G. (2008). "Naturalistic inquiry and the saturation concept: a research note." Qualitative Research **8**(1): 37-142.

Brink, C. (2010). "Quality and Standards: Clarity, Comparability and Responsibility." Quality in Higher Education **16**(2):139-152.

Bruner, R. F. and Iannarelli (2011). "Globalization of Management Education." Journal of Teaching in International Business **22**(4):232-242.

Dr. Michael Clarke

Bryman, A. (1984). "The debate about quantitative and qualitative research: a question of method or epistemology." The British Journal of Sociology **35**(1):75-92.

Bryman, A. and Bell, E. (2011). Business Research Methods (3rd edition). Oxford. Oxford University Press.

Byrne, D. (1969). "Attitudes and attraction?" In Berhowikz, L. (Ed). Advances in experimental social psychology. Academy Press. New York. **4**:35-89.

Callender, C. and Scott, P. (2013). Browne and Beyond - Modernising English Higher Education. Institute of Education Press, London.

Caluya, G., Probyn, E. and Vyas, S. (2011). "'Affective eduscapes': the case of Indian students within Australian international higher education." Cambridge Journal of Education **41**(1):85-99.

Cassel, C., Symon, G., Bvehring, A. and Johnson, P. (2006). "The role and status of qualitative research: an empirical account." Management Decision **44**(2):290-303.

Castle, R. and Kelly, D. (2010). "International education: quality assurance and standards in offshore teaching: exemplars and problems." Quality in Higher Education **10**(1):51-57.

Chambers, E. (2003). "Cultural Imperialism or Pluralism?: Cross-cultural Electronic Teaching in the Humanities." Arts and Humanities in Higher Education **2**(3):249-264.

Chan, B. T. Y. (2011). "Postgraduate transnational education in non business subjects: Can it Fit Conceptualizations of Curriculum Internationalization?" Journal of Studies in International Education **15**(3):279-298.

Chapman, A. and Pyvis, D. (2006). "Quality, identity and practice in offshore university programmes: issues in the internationalization of Australian higher education." Teaching in Higher Education **11**(2):233-245.

Chapman, D.W. and Austin, A.E. (2002). Higher Education in the Developing World. Changing contexts and Institutional Responses. Boston. Greenwood Studies in Higher Education.

Chapman, D.W. and Austin, A.E. (2002). "The Changing Context of Higher Education in the Developing World, in Chapman, D.W. and Austin, A.E. ed." Higher Education in the Developing World. Changing contexts and Institutional Responses. Boston: Centre for International Higher Education and the Program in Higher Education, 3-23.

Chapman, D., Austin, A., Farah, S., Wilson, E. and Ridge, N. (2014). "Academic Staff in the UAE: Unsettled Journey." Higher Education Policy **27:**131-151.

Cheung, P.T. (2006). "Filleting the Transnational Education Steak." Quality in Higher Education **12**(3):283-285.

Cho, J. and Trent, A. (2006). "Validity in qualitative research revisited." Qualitative Research **6:**319-340.

Chok, S.L. (2006). "'Private' and 'Public' higher education woes". New Straits Times (Malaysia). p.20.

Clark, B. (2000). "The Entrepreneurial University; New Foundations for Collegiality, Autonomy and Achievement" Journal of the Programme on Institutional Management in Higher Education **13**(2):7-24.

Clarke, M. (2012). "Challenges facing Academics in an International Branch Campus." Bath, UK, University of Bath.

Clarke, M. (2013). "Comparing 'Apples' and 'Dates': A study of the quality issues and challenges facing an International Branch Campus." Bath, UK, University of Bath.

Coleman, D. (2003). "Quality Assurance in Transnational Education." Journal of Studies in International Education **7**(4):354-378.

Connelly, S., Garton, J. and Olsen, A. (2006). "Models and Types: Guidelines for Good Practice in Transnational Education." The

Observatory Borderless Higher Education. http://www.obhe.ac.uk/ products/reports (Last accessed: 28ᵗʰ February 2013)

Coryell, J.E., Durodoyne, B.A., Wright, R.R., Pate, P.E. and Nguyen, S. (2012). "Case Studies of Internationalisation in Adult and Higher Education: Inside the Processes of Four Universities in the United States and the United Kingdom." Journal of Studies in International Education **16**(1):75-98.

Creswell, J.W. (2007). Qualitative inquiry and research design: Choosing from among five approaches. Thousand Oaks, CA. Sage.

Crichton, J. and Scarino, A. (2007). "How are we to understand the 'intercultural dimension'? An examination of the intercultural dimension of internationalization in the context of higher education in Australia." Australian Review of Applied Linguistics **30**(1):401-421.

Crossman, J. and Burdett, J. (2012). "Matters arising. Australian University Quality Agency feedback in relation to the academic engagement of international students enrolled in onshore university programmes." Quality in Higher Education **18**(2):221-234.

Crose, B. (2011). "Internationalisation of the Higher Education Classroom: Strategies to facilitate learning and academic success." International Journal of Teaching and Learning in Higher Education **23**(3):388-395.

Daniels, J. (2012). "Internationalisation, higher education and educators' perceptions of their practices." Teaching in Higher Education **18**(3):236-248.

De Meyer, A. (2012). "Reflections on the globalisation of management education." Journal of Management Development **31**(4): 336-345.

Deakin, M.K. and Sulkowski, N.B. (2007). "Does understanding culture help enhance students' learning experience?" International Journal of Contemporary Hospitality Management **21**(2):154-166.

Debowski, S. (2003). "Lost in international space: The Challenge of Sustaining Academics Teaching Offshore. Proceedings of the IDP

Conference "Securing the future for International Education." 2005, Retrieved from http://www.idp.com/17aiecpapers/speakers/article344. asp (Last accessed: 3rd January 2014).

Deem, R. (1998). "'New managerialism' and higher education: The Management of performances and cultures in universities in the United Kingdom." International Studies in Sociology of Education 8(1):47-70.

Deem, R. (2004). "The Knowledge Worker, The Manager-Academic and The Contemporary UK University: New and Old Forms of Public Management." Financial Accountability and Management 20(2):107-128.

Deardorff, D. K. (2006). "Identification and Assessment of Intercultural Competence as a Student Outcome of Internationalization." Journal of Studies in International Education 10(3):241-266.

Dearlove, J. (2002). "A Continuing Role for Academics: The Governance of UK Universities in post-Dearing Era." Higher Education Quarterly 56(3): 257-275.

Denzin, N. and Lincoln, Y. (Eds) (2000). Handbook of Qualitative Research 2nd edition, Thousand Oaks, CA: Sage.

Devitta, G. (2000). "Inclusive approaches to effective communication and active participation in the multi-cultural classroom: A international business management context." Active Learning in Higher Education 1(2):168-180.

Dobos, K. (2011). ""Serving two masters" – academics' perspectives on working at an offshore campus in Malaysia." Educational Review 63(1):19-35.

Doring, A. (2002). "Challenges to the Academic Role of Change Agent." Journal of Further and Higher Education 26(2):139-148.

Dunbar, E. (1994). "The German executive in the U.S. work and social environment: Exploring role demands." International Journal of Intercultural Relations 18:277-291.

Dunn, L. and Wallace, M. (2004). "Australian academics teaching in Singapore: striving for cultural empathy." <u>Innovations in Education and Teaching International</u> **41**(3):291-304.

Dunn, L. and Wallace, M. (2006). "Australian academics and transnational teaching: an exploratory study of their preparedness and experiences." <u>Higher Education Research and Development</u> **25**(4):357-369.

Dunne, C. (2011). "Developing an intercultural curriculum within the context of the internationalisation of higher education: terminology, typology and power." <u>Higher Education Research and Development</u> **30**(5):609-622.

Dunworth, K. (2008). "Ideas and Realities: Investigating Good Practice in the Management of Transnational English Language Programmes for the Higher Education Sector." <u>Quality in Higher Education</u> **14**(2):95-107.

Durkin, K. (2008). "The Middle Way: East Asian Masters' Students' Perceptions of Critical Argumentation in UK Universities." <u>Journal of Studies in International Education</u> **12**:38-55.

Easterby-Smith, M. (2002). <u>Management Research</u>. London. Sage.

Eastern, G. (1998). "Case Research as a Methodology for Industrial Networks: A Realist Apologia" In Naude, P. and Turnburnall, P.W. (Eds), <u>Network Dynamics in International Marketing </u>(pp. 73-87). Oxford: Pergamon.

Easton, G. (2010). "Critical realism in case study research." <u>Industrial Marketing Management</u>. **39**:118-128.

Eisenhardt, K.M. (1989). "Building theories from case study research." <u>Academy of Management Review</u> **14**(4):532-551.

El-Khawas, E. (2002) "Quality Assurance for Higher Education: Shaping Effective Policy in Developing Countries" - in Chapman, D.W. and Austin, A.E. ed. <u>Higher Education in the Developing World. Changing Contexts and Institutional Responses.</u> Boston: Centre for

International Higher Education and the Program in Higher Education, 197-215.

Eldridge, K. and Cranston, N. (2009). "Managing transnational education: does national culture really matter?" Journal of Higher Education Policy and Management **31**(1):67-79.

Ermenc, K. (2005). "Limits of the effectiveness of intercultural education and the conceptualisation of school knowledge" Intercultural Education **16**(1):41-55.

Feldman, K.A. (1987). "Research Productivity and Scholarly Accomplishment of College Teachers as Related to their Instructional Effectiveness: A Review and Exploration." Research in Higher Education. **26**(3):227-298.

Fielden, J. and Gillard, E. (2011). "A guide to offshore staffing strategies for UK universities." UK Higher Education International and Europe Unit. Research Series/7: 1-48.

Finlay, L. (2002). "Negotiating the swamp: the opportunity and challenge of reflexivity in research practice." Qualitative Research **2**(2):209-230.

Forest, J.J.F. (2010). "Globalisation, Universities and Professors." Cambridge Review of International Affairs **15**(3):435-450.

Fox, D. (1983). "Personal theories of teaching." Studies in Higher Education **8**(2):151-163.

Fraenhel, J.R., Wallen, N.E. and Hyun, H.H. (2014). How to Design and Evaluate Research in Education. New York, McGraw Hill.

Frost, N., Nolas, S.N., Brooks-Gordan, B., Esin, C., Holt, A., Mehdizadeh, L. and Shinebourne, P. (2010). "Pluralism in qualitative research: the impact of different researches and qualitative approaches on the analysis of qualitative data." Qualitative Research **10**:441-460.

Fugate, D.L. and Jefferson, R.W. (2001). "Preparing for Globalization – Do We Need Structural Change for Our Academic Programs?" Journal of Education for Business, 160-166.

Gabb, D. (2006). "Transcultural Dynamics in the Classroom." Journal of Studies in International Education 10(4):357-368.

Gappa, J.M., Austin, A.E. and Trice, A.G. (2005). "Rethinking Academic Work and Workplace." Change 37(6):32-39.

Gappa, J.M., Austin, A.E. and Trice, A.G. (2007). Rethinking Faculty Work: Higher Education's Strategies Imperative. Jossey-Bass, Wiley, San Francisco.

Gift. S., Leo-Rhynie, E. and Moniquette, J. (2006). "Quality Assurance of Transnational Education in the English-speaking Caribbean." Quality in Higher Education 12(2):125-133.

Goh, J. W. P. (2009). "Globalisation's culture consequences of MBA education across Australia and Singapore: sophistry or truth?" Higher Education 58:131-155.

Gopal, A. (2011). "Internationalisation of Higher Education: Preparing faculty to teach cross-culturally." International Journal of Teaching and Learning in Higher Education 23(3):373-381.

Gribble, K. and Ziguras, C. (2003). "Learning to Teach Offshore: Pre-Departure training for lecturers in transnational programs." Higher Education Research and Development. 22(2):206-216.

Gunasekara, C. (2007). "Pivoting the centre: reflections on undertaking qualitative interviewing in academia." Qualitative Research 7:461-475.

Halfpenny, P. (1979). "The Analysis of Qualitative Data: Sociological Review." International Journal of Qualitative Studies in Education 27:799-825.

Hamza, A. (2010). "International Experience: An opportunity for Professional Development in Higher Education." Journal of Studies in International Education 14(1):50-69.

Harding, L.M. and Lammey, R.W. (2011). "Operational Considerations for Opening a Branch Campus Abroad." New Direction for Higher Education **155**:65-78.

Hari Das, T. (1983). "Qualitative Research in Organizational Behaviour." Journal of Management Studies **20**(3):301-314.

Hassan, L. (2011). Business Research Methods. London. Sage.

Heffernan, T. and Poole, D. (2004). "Catch me I'm falling": key factors in the deterioration of offshore education partnerships." Journal of Higher Education Policy and Management **26**(1):75-90.

Helms, R. M. (2008). "Transnational Education in China: Key Challenges, Critical Issues and Strategies for Success." The Observatory on Borderless Higher Education.

Henkel, M. (1997). "Academic values and the University as Corporate Enterprise." Higher Education Quarterly **51**(2):134-143.

Hinchliffe, G.W. and Jolly, A. (2011). "Graduate identity and employability." British Educational Research Journal **37**(4):563-584.

Hoare, L. (2013). "Swimming in the deep end: transnational teaching as culture learning?" Higher Education Research and Development **32**(4):561-574.

Hodson, P.J. and Thomas, H.G. (2001). "Higher Education as an International Commodity: Ensuring quality in partnerships." Assessment & Evaluation in Higher Education **26**(2):101-112.

Hofstede, G. (1986). "Cultural Differences in Teaching and Learning." International Journal of International Relations **10**:301-320.

Hofstede, G. (1991). "Management in a multicultural society." Malaysian Management Review **26**(1):3-12.

Hughes, R. (2011). "Strategies for Managing and Leading an Academic Staff in Multiple Countries." New Directions for Higher Education **155**:19-28.

Huisman, J., de Weert, E. and Bartelse, J. (2002). "Academic careers from a European Perspective: The Declining Desirability of the Faculty Position." The Journal of Higher Education **73**(1):141-160.

Irwin, R. (2007). "Culture shock: negotiating feelings in the field." Anthropology Matters Journal **9**:1-11.

Jepsen, D. M. and Rodwell, J. J. (2008). "Convergent interviewing: a qualitative diagnostic technique for researchers." Management Research News **31**(9):650-657.

Jochems, W., Snippe, J., Smid, H.J., and Verweij, A. (1996). "The academic progress of foreign students: Study achievement and study behaviour." Higher Education **31:**325-340.

Johnson, B., & Turner, L. A. (2003). Data collection strategies in mixed methods research. In A. Tashakkori & C. Teddlie (Eds.) Handbook of mixed methods in social & behavioral research (pp. 297-320). Thousand Oaks, CA: Sage Publications.

Johnson, P. and Duberley, J. (2003). "Reflexivity in Management Research." Journal of Management Studies **40**(5):1279-1303.

Kadiwal, L. and Rind, I.A. (2013). "'Selective cosmopolitans': tutors' and students' experience of offshore higher education in Dubai." Compare: A Journal of Comparative and International Education **43**(5):689-711.

KHDA (2013). "The higher education landscape in Dubai 2012". Dubai: Knowledge and Human Development Authority.

Kim, T. and Locke, W. (2010). Transnational academic mobility and the academic profession. Centre for Higher Education Research and Information. The Open University, London.

Kinser, K. (2011). "Multinational Quality Assurance." New Directions for Higher Education **155**:53-64.

Kirk, D. (2009) "The "Knowledge Society" in the Middle East: Education and Development of Knowledge Economics." (Conference

Proceedings). Intersections of the Public and Private in Education in the GCC: 40-45.

Knight, J. (2006). Internationalisation of Higher Education: International Branch Campuses." Journal of Comparative Policy Analysis: Research and Practice **13**(4):367-381.

Knight, J. (2006). Internationalisation of Higher Education: new directions, new challenges. The 2005 IAV Global Survey Report. Paris: International Association of Universities.

Knight, J. (2011). "Education Hubs: A fad, a Brand, an Innovation?" Journal of Studies in International Education **15**(3):221-240.

Knight, J. (2013). "The changing landscape of higher education internationalisation – for better or worse?" Perspectives: Policy and Practice in Higher Education **17**(3):84-90.

Lane, J.E. (2010). "Joint Ventures in Cross-Border Higher Education: International Branch Campuses in Malaysia." In Cross Border Collaborations in Higher Education Partnerships Beyond the Classroom, edited by Chapman, D.W. and Sakamonto, R. 67-90 New York: Routledge.

Lane, J.E. (2011a). "Importing Private Higher Education: International Branch Campuses." Journal of Comparative Policy Analysis: Research and Practice **13**(4):367-381.

Lane, J.E. (2011b). "The cross-border education policy context: Education hubs, trade liberalisation, and national sovereignty." New Directions for Higher Education **2011**(155):79-85.

Lane, J.E. and Kinser.K. (2011c). "Global Expansion of International Branch Campuses: Managerial and Leadership Challenges." New Directions for Higher Education **155:** 5-17.

Lawton, L. and Katsomitros, A. (2012). "International Branch Campuses: Data and Developments." The Observatory of Borderless Higher Education.

Lawton, W., Ahmed, M., Angulo, T., Axel-Berg, A. and Burrows, A. (2013). "Horizon Scanning: what will higher education look like in 2020?" Global opportunities for UK higher education Research Series/12:1-73.

Leask, B. (2004). "Transnational Education and Intercultural learning: Reconstructing the Offshore Teaching Team to Enhance Internationalisation." Proceedings of the Australian Universities Quality Forum 2004. AUQA Occasional Publication.

Leckey, J. and Neill, N. (2001). "Quantifying Quality: The importance of student feedback." Quality in Higher Education 7(1):19-32.

Lee, B., Collier, P.M. and Culler, J. (2007). "Reflections on the use of Case Studies in the Accounting, Management and Organisational Disciplines." Qualitative Research in Organisation and Management: An International Journal 2(3):169-178.

Lim, F.C.B. (2008). "Understanding quality assurance: a cross country case study." Quality Assurance in Education 16(2):126-140.

Lim, F.C.B. (2010). "Do Too Many Rights Make a Wrong? A Qualitative Study of the Experiences of a Sample of Malaysian and Singapore Private Higher Education Providers in Transnational Quality Assurance." Quality in Higher Education 16(3):211-222.

Lincoln, Y.S. and Guba, E.G. (1985). Naturalistic Inquiry. Newbury Park. Sage.

Locke, W. and Bennion, A. (2007). "The changing academic profession in the UK and beyond". Universities UK Research Series.

Macdonald, I. (2006). "Offshore university campuses: bonus or baggage? In: critical visions: thinking, learning and researching in Higher education" - proceedings of the 2006 annual international conference of the higher education research and development society of Autralasia Inc (HERDSA), ed. A. Bunker and I. Vardi: 207-215, Perth, WA: higher education research and development society of Australasia.

Mahrous, A.A. and Ahmed, A.A. (2010). "A cross-cultural investigation of students' perceptions of the Effectiveness of Pedagogical Tools: The Middle-East, the United Kingdom and the United States." Journal of Studies in International Education **14**(3):289-306.

Mahani, S. and Molki, A. (2011). "Internationalization of Higher Education: A reflection on success and failures among foreign universities in the United Arab Emirates." Journal of International Education Research **7**(3):7-8.

Mason, G., Williams, G. and Cranmer, S. (2009). "Employability skills initiatives in higher education: what effects do they have on graduate labour market outcomes?" Education Economics **17**(1):1-30.

Mason, J. (1996). Qualitative Researching. London. Sage.

Maxwell, J.A. (2004). "Using qualitative methods for causal explanation." Field Methods **16**(3):243-264.

Maxwell, J.A. (2005). Qualitative Research Design: An Interactive Approach. Thousand Oaks, London. CA: Sage.

Mayhew, K., Deer, C. and Dua, M. (2004). "The move to mass higher education in the UK: many questions and some answers." Oxford Review of Education **30**(1):65-82.

Mazzarol, T. and Soutar, G.N. (2012). "Revisiting the global market for higher education." Asia Pacific Journal of Marketing and Logistics **24**(5):717-737.

McBurnie, G. (2000). "Quality Matters in Transnational Education: Undergoing the GATE Review Process. An Australian-Asian Case Study." Journal of Studies in International Education **4**:23-38.

McBurnie, G. and Ziguras, C. (2001)."The regulation of transnational higher education in Southeast Asia: Case studies in Hong Kong, Malaysia and Australia." Higher Education **42**:85-105.

McBurnie, G. and Ziguras, C. (2007). "Transnational Higher Education: A Stock Taking of Current Activity." <u>Journal of Studies in International Education</u> **13**(3):310-330.

McDonald, S. (2005). "Studying Actions in Context: A Qualitative Shadowing Method for Organisational Research." <u>Qualitative Research</u> **5**(4):455-473.

McMillan, J.H. (1987). "Enhancing College Students' Critical Thinking: A Review of Studies." <u>Research in Higher Education</u> **26**(1):3-29.

Mertkan-Ozunlu, S. (2007). "Reflexive accounts about qualitative interviewing within the context of educational policy in North Cyprus." <u>Qualitative Research</u> **7**:447-459.

Middlehurst, R. and Campbell, C. (2003). "Quality Assurance and Borderless Higher Education: Finding Pathways through the Maze." <u>The Observatory of Borderless Higher Education.</u>

Miles, M.B. (1979). "Qualitative Data as an Attractive Nuisance: The Problem of Analysis." <u>Administrative Science Quarterly</u> **24**(4):590-601.

Miller-Idriss, C. and Hanauer, E. (2011). "Transnational Higher Education: Offshore campuses in the Middle East." <u>Comparative Education</u> **47**(2):181-207.

Montgomery, C. (2009). "A Decade of Internationalisation: Has It Influenced Students' Views of Cross-Cultural Group Work at University?" <u>Journal of Studies in International Education</u> **13**(2):256-270.

Morgan, G. and Smircich, L. (1980). "The Case for Quality Research." <u>Academy of Management Review</u> **5**:491-500.

Moussly, R. (2012). "Academic cheating is a serious problem in the UAE, researcher finds." Gulf news. [online] Retrieved from: <u>http://www.gulfnews.com/Education</u> (Last accessed: 19th August 2012).

Naidoo, R. (2003). "Repositioning Higher Education as a Global Commodity: Opportunities and Challenges for future sociology of education work." British Journal of Sociology of Education **24**(2):249-259.

Naidoo, R. (2007). "Higher Education as a Global Commodity: The Perils and Promises for Developing Countries. The Observatory on Borderless Higher Education. 1-19.

Naidoo, R. (2011). "Rethinking development: higher education and the new imperialism" in King, R.; Marginson, S.; Naidoo, R. Ed. Handbook on Globalisation and Higher Education. Cheltenham, UK.

Naidoo, V. (2009). "Transnational Higher Education: A stock take of Current Activity." Journal of Studies in International Education, **13**:310-330.

Napier, N. K., Anh, V.D., Thang, N.V. and Tuan, V.V. (1997). "Reflections on Building a Business School in Vietnam - Falling Into an Opportunity for Making a Difference." Journal of Management Inquiry **6**(4):341-354.

Ndiweni, E. and Verhoeven, H. (2012) "Academic Expatriates: learning how to make scones but still eating Umm Ali? Expanding Knowledge or commodification of labour and education." Paper presented at the International Conference of Critical Accounting, New York, USA.

Nieto, C. and Booth, M.Z. (2010). "Cultural Competence: Its Influence on the Teaching and Learning of International Students." Journal of Studies in International Education **14**(4):406-425.

O'Leary, Z. (2004). The Essential Guide to Doing Research. London. Sage.

O'Reilly, M. and Parker, N. (2013). "Unsatisfactory saturation: a critical exploration of the notion of saturated sample sizes in qualitative research." Qualitative Research **13**:190-197.

Oberg, K. (1960). "Culture shock: adjustment to new cultural environments." Practical Anthropology **7**:177-182.

Onwuegbuzie, A.J. (2003). "Expanding the framework of internal and external validity in quantitative research." Research in the Schools 10:71-90.

Onwuegbuzie, A.J. and Leech, N.L. (2007). "Validity and Qualitative Research: An Oxymoron?" Quality and Quantity 41:233-249.

Panteli, N. and Tucker, R. (2009). "Power and Trust in Global Virtual Teams." Communications of the ACM 52(12):113-115.

Parker, M. and Jary, D. (1995). "The McUniversity Organisation, Management and Academic Subjectivity." Organisations 2(2):319-338.

Patton, M. Q. (2002). Qualitative Research and Evaluation Methods. (3rd edition). Thousand Oaks. CA. Sage.

Pedró, F. (2009). "Continuity and Change in the Academic Profession in European countries." Higher Education in Europe 34(3-4):411-429.

Piekkari, R., Welch, C. and Paavilainen, E. (2009). "Case Study as Disciplinary Convention: Evidence from International Business Journals." Organisational Research Methods 12(3):567-589.

Piercy, N.E., Harris, C.C. and Lane, N. (2002). "Market Orientation and Retail Operatives Expectations." Journal of Business Research 55:261-273.

Poole, D. and Ewan, C. (2010). "Academics as part-time marketers in university offshore programs: an exploratory study." Journal of Higher Education Policy & Management 32(2):149-158.

Porter, P. and Vidovich, L. (2000). "Globalization and Higher Education Policy." Educational Theory 50(4):449-465.

Porter, S. (2007). "Validity, trustworthiness and rigour: reassuring realism in qualitative research." Journal of Advanced Nursing 60(1):79-86.

Pyvis, D. (2011). "The need for context-sensitive measures of educational quality in transnational higher education." Teaching in Higher Education 16(6):733-744.

Pyvis, D. and Chapman, A. (2005). "Culture shock and the international student 'offshore'." Journal of Research in International Education 4(1):23-42.

Quality Assurance Agency. (2012). "Review of transnational education in Mainland China 2012". Gloucester, UK.

Quality Assurance Agency. (2014). "Review of UK Transnational Education in United Arab Emirates: Overview". Gloucester, UK.

Ratcliffe, R. (2013). "Rise in UK degrees abroad." Gulf News (dated 16th February 2013).

Rawazik, W. and Carroll, M. (2009). "Complexity in Quality Assurance in a Rapidly Growing Free Economic Environment: A UAE Case Study." Quality in Higher Education 15(1):79-83.

Riach, K. (2009). "Exploring Participant-Centered Reflexivity in the Research Interview." Sociology 43(2):356-370.

Richardson, J. (2000). "Expatriate Academics in the Globalized Era: The Beginnings of an Untold Story?" Asia Pacific Business Review 7(1):125-150.

Richardson, J. (2008). The Independent Expatriate: Academics Abroad. A Study of Expatriate Academics in New Zealand, Singapore, the United Arab Emirates and Turkey VDM Verlag Dr. Müller. Saarbrucken, Germany.

Richardson, J. and Mallon, M. (2005). "Career interrupted? The case of the self-directed expatriate." Journal of World Business 40:409-420.

Richardson, J. and McKenna, S. (2002). "Learning and experiencing: why academics expatriate and how they experience expatriation." Career Development International 7(2):67-78.

Richardson, J. and McKenna, S. (2003). "International experience and academic careers: What do academics have to say?" Personnel Review 32(6):774-795.

Richardson, J. and Zikic, J. (2007). "The darker side of an international academic career." Career Development International **12**(2):164-186.

Roberts, R., Wallace, W. and O'Farrell P. (2009). Introduction to Business Research 1. CAPDM Ltd. Edinburgh.

Robson, S. (2001). "Internationalization: a transformative agenda for higher education?" Teachers and Teaching: Theory and Practice **17**(6):619-630.

Roulston, K., DeMarrais, K. and Lewis, J.B. (2003). "Learning to Interview in the Social Sciences." Qualitative Inquiry **9**:643-668.

Salmi, J. (2002). "Higher Education at a Turning Point", in Chapman, D.W. and Austin, A.E. ed. Higher Education in the Developing World. Changing Contexts and Institutional Responses. Boston: Centre for International Higher Education and the Program in Higher Education, 23-41.

Salt, J. and Wood. P (2014) "Staffing UK University Campuses Overseas: Lessons from MNE Practice". Journal of Studies in International Education. **18**(1): 84-97.

Sanderson, G. (2008). "A foundation for the Internationalisation of the Academic Staff." Journal of Studies in International Education **12**:276-307.

Schapper, J.M. and Mayson, S.E. (2004). "Internationalisation of Curricula: An alternative to the Taylorisation of academic work." Journal of Higher Education Policy and Management **26**(2):189-205.

Schermerhorn, J. R. J. (1999). "Learning by Going? The Management Educator as Expatriate." Journal of Management Inquiry **8**(3):246-256.

Scheurich, J.J. (1997). Research Method in the Postmodern. London and Philadephia: PA; Routledge and Falmer.

Schoorman, D. (2000). "The Pedagogical Implications of Diverse Conceptualisations of Internationalisation: A U.S. case study." Journal of Studies in International Education, **3**(2):19-46.

Schoorman, D. (2000). "What really do we mean "internationalization"? Education **71**:5-11.

Scott, P. (2000). "Globalisation and Higher Education: Challenges for the 21st Century." Journal of Studies in International Education **4**(1):3-10.

Seale, C. (1999). The Quality of Qualitative Research. London. Sage.

Selmer, J. and Lauring, J. (2009). "Cultural similarity and adjustment of expatriate academics." International Journal of Intercultural Relations **33**:429-436.

Selmer, J. and Lauring, J. (2011). "Expatriate academics: job factors and work outcomes." International Journal of Manpower **32**(2):194-210.

Shams, F. and Huisman, J. (2012). "Managing Offshore Branch Campuses: An Analytical Framework for Institutional Strategies." Journal of Studies in International Education **16**(2):106-127.

Shore, C. and Wright, S. (2000). "Coercive accountability: the rise of audit culture in higher education." In Strathern, M. Audit Cultures. Anthropological studies in accountability, ethics and the academy. Routledge Abingdon. New York.

Signorini, P., Wiesemes, R. and Murphy, R. (2009). "Developing alternative frameworks for exploring intercultural learning: a critique of Hofstede's cultural difference model." Teaching in Higher Education **14**(3):253-264.

Silverman, D. (ed) (2004). Qualitative Research: Theory, Method and Practice. 2nd edition. London. Sage.

Sims, R. and Schraeder, M. (2004). "An examination of salient factors affecting expatriate culture shock." Journal of Business and Management **1**(1):73-88.

Sin, C. H. (2005). "Seeking Informed Consent: Reflections on Research Practice." Sociology **39**(2):277-294.

Smith, J.K. (1983). "Quantitative versus Qualitative Research: An attempt to clarify the issue." Educational Researcher **12**:6-13.

Smith, L. (2006). "Teachers' conceptions of teaching at a Gulf university: A starting point for revising a teacher development program". Learning and Teaching in Higher Education: Gulf Perspectives **3**(1): 4-13.

Smith, L. (2009). "Sinking in the sand? Academic work in an offshore campus of an Australian university." Higher Education Research & Development **28**(5):467-479.

Smith, K. (2009). "Transnational teaching experiences: an under-explored territory for transformative professional development." International Journal for Academic Development **14**(2):111-122.

Smith, K. (2010). "Assuring quality in transnational higher education: a matter of collaboration or control?" Studies in Higher Education **35**(7):793-806.

Spencer, L., Richie, J., Lewis, J. and Dillon, L. (2003). Quality in Qualitative Evaluation: A framework for Assessing Research Evidence. London: Government Chief Social Researcher's Office.

Stella, A. (2006). "Quality Assurance of Cross-border Higher Education." Quality in Higher Education **12**(3):257-276.

Storen, L.A. and Aamodt, P.O. (2010). "The quality of higher education and employability of graduates." Quality in Higher Education **16**(3):297-313.

Strauss, A. (1987). Qualitative analysis for social scientists. Cambridge, UK: Cambridge University Press.

Strauss, A. and Corbin, J. (1990). Basics of Qualitative Research: Grounded Theory Procedures and Techniques. Newbury Park, CA: Sage.

Strauss, A. and Corbin, J. (1998). Basics of qualitative research, techniques and procedures for developing grounded theory. 2nd Edition. London: Sage.

Sulkowski, N.B. and Deakin, M.K. (2009). "Does understanding culture help enhance students' learning experience?" International Journal of Contemporary Hospitality Management **21**(2):154-166.

Takeda, A. (2013). "Reflexivity: unmarried Japanese male interviewing married Japanese women about international marriage." Qualitative Research **13**:285-298.

Tam, M. (2001). "Measuring Quality and Performance in Higher Education." Quality in Higher Education **7**(1):47-54.

Tan, L. T. (2010). "Towards a culturally sensitive and deeper understanding of "Rote Learning" and memorisation of adult learners." Journal of Studies in International Education **15**:124-145.

Teekens, H. (2003). "The Requirement to Develop Specific Skills for Teaching is an Intercultural Setting." Journal of Studies in International Education **7**:108-119.

Thorn, K. (2009). "The relative importance of motives for international self-initiated mobility." Career Development International **14**(5): 441-464.

Tight, M. (2010). "The Curious Case of Case Study: a Viewpoint." International Journal of Social Research Methodology **13**(4):329-339.

Trahar, S. and Hyland, F. (2011). "Experiences and perceptions of internationalisation in higher education in the UK." Higher Education Research and Development **30**(5):623-633.

Tsang, E.W.K. (2013). "Case study methodology: causal explanation, contextualization and theorizing." Journal of International Management **19:** 195-202.

UAE National Bureau of Statistics (2001) www.uaestatistics.gov.ae (Last accessed: 7th July 2014)

Van Damme, D. (2001). "Quality issues in the internationalisation of higher education." Higher Education **41**:415-441.

Van Der Wende, M. (1999). "Quality Assurance of Internationalisation and Internationalisation of Quality Assurance." Organisation for Economic Co-operation and Development 225-239.

Wallace, M. and Wray, A. (2011). Critical Reading and Writing for Postgraduates. London: Sage.

Ward, W., Bocker, S. and Furnham, A. (2001) The Psychology of Culture Shock. Routeledge. London.

Waring, M. A. (2010). "Moments of Vision: HRM and the Individualisation of Academic Workers." PhD Thesis submitted to the University of Wales. Cardiff.

Welch, A. (1998). "The End of Certainty? The Academic Profession and the Challenge of Change." Comparative Education Review 42(1):1-14.

Welch, R.A. (1997). "The peripatetic professor: the internationalisation of the academic profession." Higher Education 34:323-345.

Whalley, T. (1997). "Best practice guidelines for internationalizing the curriculum." Douglas College for the Province of British Columbia of Education, Skills and Training, and the Centre for Curriculum, Transfer and Technology.

Wilkins, S. (2010). "Higher Education in the United Arab Emirates: an analysis of the outcomes of significant increases in supply and competition." Journal of Higher Education Policy & Management 32(4):389-400.

Wilkins, S. and Huisman, J. (2011). "Student Recruitment at International Branch Campuses: can they compete in the Global Market?" Journal of Studies in International Education 15(3):299-316.

Wilkins, S., Balakrishnan, M.S. and Huisman, J. (2012). "Student satisfaction and student perceptions of quality at international branch campuses in the United Arab Emirates." Journal of Higher Education Policy and Management 34(5):543-556.

Wilkinson, R. and Yussof, L. (2005). "Public and private provision of higher education in Malaysia: A comparative analysis". Higher Education. **50**:361-386.

Williams, M. (2000). "Interpretivism and Generalisation." Sociology **34**:209-224.

Willmott, H. (1995). "Managing the Academics: Commodification and Control in the Development of University Education in the UK." Human Relations **48:**993-1027.

Winston, G.C. (1994). "The decline in undergraduate teaching: moral failure or market pressure?" Change **26**(5):8-15.

Woolf, M. (2002). "Harmony and Dissonance in International Education: The limits of Globalisation." Journal of Studies in International Education **6**(5):5-15.

Woodhouse, D. (2006). "The Quality of Transnational Education: A provider view." Quality in Higher Education **12**(3):277-281.

Woodhouse, D. and Stella, A. (2008). "Borderless Higher Education 'Down Under' Quality Assurance of Australian Cross-Border Initiatives." The Observatory of Borderless Higher Education. http://www.obhe.ac.uk/products/reports/ (Last accessed: 2nd March 2013)

Xian, H. (2008). "Lost in Translation? Language Culture and the Roles of Translator in Cross-Cultural Management Research." Qualitative Research in Organisations and Management **3**(3):231-245.

Yilmaz, K. (2013). "Comparison of Quantitative and Qualitative Research Traditions: epistemological, theoretical and methodological differences." European Journal of Education **48**(2):311-325.

Yin, R.K. (2009). Case study research: design and methods. Thousand Oaks, CA. Sage.

Zhang, Y. and Mi, Y. (2010). "Another Look at the Language Difficulties of International Students." Journal of Studies in International Education **14**(4):371-388.

Printed in the United States
By Bookmasters